Praise for Can

"Can You Keep A Secret" is, a groundbreaking, insightful, courageous and honest portrayal of child abuse and human trafficking in today's populace. Headley shares some difficult lessons learned in her journey to find the truth about the debilitating effect of the victims who do not fit into the neat categorical behaviors owing to exploitation of family, employers, caregivers, or cultural norms. This ... is engaging, confronting, practically relevant, boldly challenging... fascinating read. Be sure to share it with your friends."

Rev. Joshua A McClure, Th.D.,
Pastor (Retired), Author "My Learning Library. (9) Books, Christian Educator, Publisher, Radio host

"The book is conversational, written lucidly and boldly challenging the reader to something so simple but so unconventional that I was forced to go back and re-read several times the statements that the author makes, just by asking this implicitly loaded question - the title of this book. 'Can You Keep A Secret?' sounds as if someone is inviting you to be a conspirator; alluring to be part of something tantalizing or even enticing..."

Brinda Adige, Founder and Mentor,
Global Concerns India, Bangalore

i

"Her book, 'Can You Keep A Secret?' draws you in and doesn't let go until the closing sentence... Her real life stories will keep you on the edge of your seat.... This book is a must read for anyone, or any organization, that is interested in confronting, and reversing, the horrible plagues of child sexual exploitation and human trafficking in our culture and world. Please, please, you must read this book!"

Larry Dershem, Esq. President,
National Law Center for Children and Families

"Juanita uniquely and transparently shares her heart; her faith; and her calling to speak out against, what many consider to be this generations most horrific injustice, human trafficking and sexual abuse..."

Doug Dworak, Executive Director,
Love Justice International

"Juanita is relentless with her passion and fearlessness about bringing child sexual abuse and its linkages to commercial sexual exploitation from the shadows. By honestly sharing her own secret, Juanita illustrates the importance of understanding the difference between keeping and telling secrets.... We all have a role to protect the Juanitas' in the world from abuse and violence. Our obligation starts today."

Nicole G. Epps, Managing Director,
World Childhood Foundation (WCF)

"Juanita Headley bursts upon the pages of this book much like her life is exploding into this unjust world, battling the plague of human trafficking from Asia to the Americas and then to Europe. She is a warrior armed with an unmovable belief in her mission and energized by a holy calling."

Thomas Estler, Founder and Director,
Freedom Ladder

"While we know there is no easy or 'quick fix,' this book gives realistic suggestions and answers on how to handle a situation which can be equated to modern day slavery. We have a moral imperative to address the situation.... I urge you to take Juanita's lead, be aware and make a difference. Not every secret is meant to be kept..."

Honorable Rhonda Fischer, Acting County Court Judge,
District Court of Nassau County

"A survivor testimonial that is a must read. It highlights the power of vulnerability and has strategies to combat sexual abuse from lived experience. Nothing can be more useful for those wishing to confront child sexual abuse and grooming."

Professor Ruchira Gupta, Founder and President,
Apne Aap Women Worldwide

"Juanita is a passionate advocate for victims of child sexual abuse and human trafficking. 'Can You Keep A Secret?' is a very honest account of her life and experiences around the world and will provide valuable information to those seeking to assist in the restoration of those suffering in silence."

Tim Hughes, Country Director,
She Rescue Home

"Juanita Headley has written a must-read for anyone who thinks trafficking is not happening in his or her own community."

Chris Hunt, President,
The Lily & The Sparrow

"Juanita's story is refreshingly honest and authentic. She writes from the heart and demonstrates a sacrificial commitment to helping others. Juanita has experienced darkness and hopelessness; she has not allowed her past to crush her but instead has responded with a message of hope for others and a determination not to give up no matter what the cost."

Greg Malstead, Co-Founder,
Freedom Firm

"Juanita Headley is a warrior on the front lines of fighting the trafficking of young people. Her book will add immeasurably to our understanding of this problem and our urgency to fight it."

Patricia McCormick,
Author of SOLD

"Attorney Juanita Headley is the most dedicated person I know in the fight against global human trafficking. 'Can You Keep A Secret?' gives you an unprecedented look into the world of human trafficking, it will inspire you to get involved in the movement of abolishing the ancient practices of human slavery and trafficking worldwide."

Doctor Stephany Powell, Executive Director,
Journey Out

"Kudos to Juanita Headley with her tireless efforts to bring awareness to childhood sexual abuse and human trafficking. Her excellent book chronicles her passion and provides behavioral indicators for all of us to be aware of."

Nancy Rivard, President and Founder,
Airline Ambassadors International

"Juanita Headley is a passionate and fascinating human being with a heart for combating human exploitation around the globe. She goes where few of us would be willing to go. She has an entrepreneurial mind and a

missionary's heart. Trained as a legal professional, she is able to share her insights and expertise in a unique and engaging way…. The reader is sure to find the story of her personal journey from London to New York to Trinidad a fascinating read. Be sure to share it with your friends."

Opal Singleton, President and CEO, **Million Kids**

Can You Keep A Secret?

BY
ATTORNEY
JUANITA MAUD HEADLEY

Published by
Forward Thinking Publishing

ISBN: 978-1-7397230-3-3

Book design by Robert Rollocks, imreflections@gmail.com Author photograph by Rick James of Make it Happen Production All photographs by Julia Boyd unless otherwise credited

Second Edition 2022

Scripture quotations from The Authorized (King James) Version. Rights in the Authorized Version in the United Kingdom are vested in the Crown. Reproduced by permission of the Crown's patentee, Cambridge University Press.

Scriptures taken from the Holy Bible, New International Version®, NIV®. Copyright © 1973, 1978, 1984, 2011 by Biblica, Inc.™ Used by permission of Zondervan. All rights reserved worldwide. www. zondervan.com The "NIV" and "New International Version" are trademarks registered in the United States Patent and Trademark Offi ce by Biblica, Inc.™

Permission to Quote from CYKAS: *Can You Keep A Secret?* Must be directed to Juanita Maud Headley, Juanita.headley@changingcases.com.

A catalogue record for this book is available from the British Library

Visit the author's website at www.changingcases.org.

Published by Forward Thinking Publishing

To "He who finds a wife"[1] and finds me.

To Rev. William Abaiku Apprey for teaching me Christ's forgiveness[2]; and becoming the biggest blessing that Ghana has to offer to me; Richard Dunkley for his never-ending kindness, dedication, sacrifice and commitment, without his help, 3 years later this book would still not be on Amazon; and Zdenka Safarova, the most selfless individual I have ever met.

I love you all very much and wish there were more people in the world as generous, consistent and dependable as each of you.

---

[1] *"He who finds a wife finds a good thing."* (Proverbs 18:22)

[2] *"Then Peter came to Jesus and asked, "Lord, how many times shall I forgive my brother or sister who sins against me? Up to seven times?" Jesus answered, "I tell you, not seven times, but seventy-seven times."* Matthew 18:21-22 (New International Version)

Contents

To Joy
May you be educated
and empowered by
His book. God bless
you all.   Oct 27
                   2022

Foreword

With the passion of Christ by her side Juanita Maud Headley has delivered a gripping tale of her story of redemption and justice in 'Can You Keep A Secret?' Her writing has the clarity of the seasoned lawyer she is and the fire of a survivor of the darkest aspects of human behavior.

I met Juanita at the Hollywood premiere of SOLD. Immediately I was struck by her tenacity and commitment to this issue. She has an incredible heart and I am proud to support her.

She is a champion for human decency and a relentless savior in her own right. 'Can You Keep A Secret?' Asks the reader to reply, "Yes" and if I was asked if you should read this book I would reply "Yes" as well.

Picture taken by Julia Boyd of MS Media TV

I applaud her for the brilliant concise writing, her undying drive to stand up for the underdog and her bright light of a heart.

David Arquette
Hollywood Actor, SOLD

Preface

I accepted an invitation to appear as a panelist on the program, "Ask Why?" alongside Alloy Youk See and Rochelle Nakhid for a human trafficking discussion on Catholic station Trinity T.V. On the evening of July 24th, 2018, I appeared on the show not as prepared as I would have liked, but I was excited, nonetheless, about the opportunity.

This would have been my first televised panel discussion and I had no idea what to expect. In fact, despite the weeks of preparation that I could have utilized beforehand, the whole idea had initially really daunted me. My fear was centered on the types of questions the audience might ask and whether I would have the expertise to answer them. Fortunately, that night only two viewers called in and neither one of them posed a question.

My co-panelist, Alloy had posed the question, "Can you tell a secret?" and had asked me to explain it to the audience. In fact, the question had been "Can You Keep A Secret?" and it was the third most important topic of discussion. Aside from sharing my own personal story of childhood sexual abuse, and my faith in Jesus Christ, I would always bring this question up during my interviews.

As Alloy drove me home that night, I thanked him for bringing up the question. I had no clue at the time that just a few days later an idea would formulate in my mind of writing a book titled, "Can You Keep A Secret?" to enable my message to reach a wider audience than just the nation of Trinidad and Tobago but, in fact, the entire world.

Although at face value it was a seemingly simple question, it frequently got overcomplicated, therefore I decided to embark on a journey to educate the public on the issues of child abuse and human trafficking in what would be an easy to read format.

I decided to make this book conversational by taking entire excerpts from my human trafficking presentation and placing it in text form. Although I had never used a written script for my presentations, through the use of pictures I had developed a mental script that I would repeat verbatim every time I spoke. Thus, this book would be the firstopportunity not only for me, but also for you, the reader, to get full access to the written transcript of my presentation.

Juanita Maud Headley.
July 2018.

Acknowledgments

First and foremost, I would like to thank my Lord and Savior Jesus Christ who used circumstances and people to inspire me to finally put pen to paper. Whilst juggling a somewhat hectic speaking engagement schedule and with a completion date of a month, it was truly a blessing to have accomplished the impossible in such a short period of time and was indeed nothing short of a miracle.

The completion of my first book has been a very long time coming and I am grateful to all the people who encouraged me to share my story. I possess the gift of storytelling and am thrilled to share a part of my journey with the rest of the world.

It is truly a great honor to express my utmost gratitude to attorney William Hollberg and aspiring attorney Zdenka Safarova, without whose help, immeasurable sacrifice and investment this book would not have been published. Likewise, the selfless dedication of Robert Rollocks who designed this book cover without charge; and Jacob Aureus for providing additional financial assistance for the formatting of this book.

I am also grateful to New York attorney Kenneth Landau who has been more like an uncle than a mentor to me. His sincerity, generosity and thoughtfulness over the last five years have been incredibly touching and I love him very much.

I take pride in acknowledging Rosa Fraticelli who has consistently lent an ear to me without 'ear tickling'[3] but always spoke the truth with love and respect, and maintained a positive, non-judgmental approach throughout all of our interactions. She is the only person I know that has never claimed that her opinion was fact in my situation, but instead she has always directed me to God for a solution. Despite the number of years that passed between the times that we would physically meet or have a verbal conversation this never diminished our communication because unlike so many others she never allowed distance to separate us.

I would also like to express my sincere gratitude to two amazing web designers: Kyle Grant, CEO of Grant Distributors (service@grantdistributors.com), and Gabriel Konadu Boateng (iboateng777@gmail.com). Their selflessness, dedication, commitment, loyalty and generosity have been immeasurable and for the first time have made these words take meaning in my life, "Appreciate the people who give you their free time, but truly value the people who free their time for you."

I would like to thank Naseem Nurse for providing complimentary makeovers for the author photo, and photographer Rick James from 'Make it Happen'

---

[3] *"For the time will come when people will not put up with sound doctrine. Instead, to suit their own desires, they will gather around them a great number of teachers to say what their itching ears want to hear." 2 Timothy 4:3 (NIV)*

Production for donating countless hours to take the author photos and videos.

I would also like to thank all of the people who blessed me along my journey these past six years, extending a hand of generosity to me albeit me being a complete stranger to them. There are simply too many names to mention here, but they all know who they are. Thank you for your support, prayer, protection and provision.

My acknowledgment would be incomplete without thanking my late best friend Minerva Stevens who was a tremendous source of support toward me throughout my teenage years. She provided me with consistent emotional support no matter where I was in the world and my life has never been the same without her.

Finally, thank you the reader of this book for making this financial investment that will enable my dreams to become a reality. May this book transform your thoughts and perceptions, may you experience freedom and fulfillment and be truly blessed by the words that I have taken the time to write on each page.

Introduction

If someone comes up to you and asks, "Can you keep a secret?" would you answer, "YES," "NO" or "IT DEPENDS?" Think about this question for a minute.

Now, let me ask you, was your immediate, confident response, "It depends?"

Whenever I would ask my audience this question over 90% would confidently answer, "It depends." That left a handful responding "No" and an even smaller amount answering, "Yes."

I want you to understand that from this day forward, the answer to that question must always be "Yes" or something else affirmative. Let me explain why. Whenever someone comes up to you and says, "Can you keep a secret?" or a different variation of that question such as "Can you keep this between us?" or "Will this be confidential?" those questions all signify a cry for help or that they are trying to tell you something sensitive.

Now consider a scenario where you respond, "No" or "It depends" when asked the question, "Can you keep a secret?" The individual who approached you would simply (figuratively speaking) keep on walking. They may, however, come back to you weeks, months or even years later and ask you that very same question because they would be hoping for a different response. However, if you still said, "No" or "It depends," then once again they would leave without making their disclosure.

So, let's try that again; if someone comes up to you and says, "Can you keep a secret?" this time you say, "Yes" or something else affirmative such as, "Tell me your secret, what is your secret?", or "I can listen to your secret." By responding in that way, the person should then feel comfortable enough to confide in you and may say something like "I'm being sexually abused by my uncle."

Once you've heard their revelation, you now have the responsibility to inform the individual, if necessary, of your next steps of intervention by saying something such as, "I apologize but I have to break your trust," and ONLY then do you call the police.

Now there is no script as to the exact words that you should use, but you need to say something primarily to prevent trust issues. The idea of breaking the individual's trust is in fact something that some people initially really do wrestle with because it seems to be a kind of betrayal. That is really not so. In my opinion, if a person has disclosed a current situation of abuse, then immediate intervention is never up for discussion. Likewise, the possibility of the person developing trust issues would be the least of my concerns in instances such as that. However, to minimize the likelihood of that occurring, there needs to be a conversation that takes place.

Introduction

In some, but not all instances, the perpetrator of the abuse told the victim that if the perpetrator was exposed, the police would arrest the victim; therefore, if the victim was unprepared for what would happen next, when confronted by the police, out of fear they could recant their accusation, attempt to pretend the abuse didn't happen or in some rare cases commit suicide.

The possibility of the victim committing suicide was an issue presented by a number of audience participants who feared that by 'breaking the victim's trust,' the victim would take their own life. Again, I believe, that this is a risk you have the responsibility to take. When a person discloses abuse, instead of considering all of the 'what-ifs' of how your intervention may or may not indirectly cause harm or embarrassment to that person, I believe that the focus should instead be on removing them from the abusive situation and if concerns of suicide are really genuine, then the individual should be placed on suicide watch.

The mistaken belief has been that suicide watch only exists inside prison, however, that does not necessarily have to be the case. In a situation where there are fears that the abused individual is suicidal, their parents, guardians or family members should be put on alert to remove all dangerous items from that person's reach. This includes but is not limited to razors, mirrors, sleeping pills, shoelaces, belts, ropes, scissors, knives etc., or anything else with a sharp or pointy edge or with the ability to inflict self-harm.

Now assuming, as it is common in the vast majority of situations, that the individual is not suicidal after their disclosure of abuse to you, you must inform them of the next steps you are now obligated to take to protect them. Following which, you would begin taking those steps by informing the appropriate authorities.

It is all very simple in theory, but the reality is that it really isn't that easy, more so because there are people who struggle with replying "Yes" because they feel it is misleading or dishonest. In my career, albeit I am not paid to function as a professional liar, I mean professional lawyer, it has been very easy for me to respond affirmatively to this question.

Here's why when a person asks, "Can you keep a secret?" I would respond, "Yes," because I could keep that secret, a least for about a minute. The person tells me their secret and then I begin mentally counting down "59, 58, 57...." Okay, not literally, but the point is I could keep that secret. I would listen to their secret, explain to them the next steps and only then, would I break the trust of keeping that secret.

As a young adult in my audience once said, "I said I can keep a secret, but I did not say that I will." I know, I know, there are still some of you who feel like you're being misleading, but if you look at the bigger picture, ask yourself, "Does it really matter? Is it really that serious when there is a victim right in front of you that needs your immediate help and intervention?"

Outside of my profession, as a practicing Christian I do not believe that saying, "Yes" is a lie for the reasons I

4

have just explained. In my own life, as a result of getting "It depends" from two different family members, I believe that I am healed in Jesus name, but I used to be insecure; I used to have low self-esteem; I used to have few friends; I used to wet the bed; I used to have anger issues; I used to have insomnia ... the list is endless.

On the other hand, I believe that if I had received the answer "Yes," then I would have been married by now, with an orphanage in the Philippines and two adopted Filipino street children. Instead, as a result of the "It depends," I would travel around the world giving free presentations in what could best be described as my bid to find my healing.

Realistically speaking, I should be paid to speak on human trafficking and the solicitations should be coming to me and not from me. Instead, I have been perceived by some as a transient with no expertise on human trafficking, with no life outside of speaking engagements and desperate to get some air time. Nothing could be further from the truth, but my passion and persistence was sometimes ill-perceived. Few people truly understood my value, not as an attorney, but simply as a human being, a person worthy and deserving of genuine respect.

My worth should never be determined by how much it costs to have me speak at an engagement or function (which came priced at a mere $0.00), because the information that I provide has always far exceeded its free price tag. Those individuals who had the opportunity to hear my presentation would immediately understand my value albeit sometimes momentarily. One person who comes to mind is an employee of the Criminal Records Office - Crime Scene Unit in Port of Spain, Trinidad; at the conclusion of my presentation he remarked, "I have paid money to attend presentations and wanted a refund and you do this for free!!"

Those were the most affirming words I had ever been told concerning my free presentations. Someone actually got it! But, for the first time more importantly, so did I. From that day forward, those words remained imprinted in my mind. Once again, if I had indeed got a "Yes" response all those years ago I would not have needed an employee of the Criminal Records Office - Crime Scene Unit to tell me my value because I would have known it all along.

So whenever people would cancel on me at the last minute, or I was blatantly disrespected or blocked for no justifiable reason, I would remind myself that I had value and that my value was not determined by the number of dollar bills I had in my hand at the end of a presentation.

I am not, nor have I ever been cheap or desperate. I am a law-abiding citizen, unwilling to get a salary for my presentations in the absence of a work permit. That work permit is certainly on its way and would signify an upgrade in my means of operation. No longer would my life be dictated to by speaking engagements, nor would my meals be few and far between, but instead, I would have the flexibility and freedom that comes with financial provision, and a cancellation policy that ensures whether or not I spoke I would still eat.

Afford me your cooperation for a moment, just for the sake of emphasis, for those of you who are still a "No" or "It depends." I want you to try this interactive activity with me by reading the next few lines and following the instructions:

1. Think of a man or woman, boy or girl that you love and care about.

2. I want you to close your eyes and picture this individual for a minute before opening your eyes and reading step three.

3. I want you to imagine that person comes up to you and says, "Can you keep a secret?" You reply, "It depends" or "No." How would you feel if they smuggled drugs between two countries and ended up murdered or in jail?

4. Close your eyes and visualize that scenario for a minute before opening your eyes again.

5. Now I want you to think of that man or woman, boy or girl that you love and care about. They come up to you and say, "Can you keep a secret?" You respond, "It depends," or "No." How would you feel if they commit suicide tomorrow?

6. Close your eyes and visualize that situation for a minute and then open your eyes.

7. Ask yourself, how would you feel? What is your most honest answer? Sad, maybe guilty or self-blame?

Can You Keep A Secret?

Whenever my audience would respond to this rhetorical question they would say things like sad, horrible or guilty. Now remember this is only a hypothetical situation but imagine putting this book down and one of those two situations actually played out right now in your life. I'm sure that would initially be very scary since you had just gone through this activity, but aside from that initial shock you would probably experience a lot of regret.

My desire for you is that you never have to experience the reality of either of those two hypotheses; but instead for you to be your 'brother's keeper' - in the very general sense of the word ... and who is your brother? That would be your neighbor, colleague, or even a complete stranger that you sit beside on your commute to work.

Let me explain something for those of you who still have not been swayed to answer "Yes" to "Can you keep a secret?"

At the age of four, my mother's husband tried to rape me. As a result of the "It depends," although I have been healed in Jesus name, I used to suffer from low self-esteem; insecurity; anger issues; etc. If I had instead gotten a "Yes," I would have received therapy or counseling years earlier, I would be mentally healthy and whole, and I would be contentedly married with an orphanage in the Philippines and adopted children.

Whenever someone poses the question, "Can you keep a secret?" you should ALWAYS answer "Yes" with your mouth and "It depends" in your head.

Let me say that again, and I want you to internalize what I'm saying with the knowledge of my truth and the understanding of the lingering trauma that could have been avoided. At the age of four my mother's husband tried to take my virginity. It CANNOT be an "It depends," it's non- negotiable! You say "Yes" with your mouth and "It depends" in your head.

Let me say that again, at four my mother's husband tried to rape me. It cannot, SHOULD NOT, MUST NOT EVER be an "It depends."

If, after everything you read in this book, you are still a "No" or an "It depends," then I am truly scared for your family. I'm scared for your sons, I'm scared for your daughters, and I'm scared for your nieces and nephews.

Please do not think that you're smarter than the author of this book, because on this point, you are not! Taking into account everything else you will read here, I give you permission to disregard or disagree with me. I am completely okay with that because this is the most important information you can take away from this book. It is ALWAYS a "Yes" with your mouth and "It depends" in your head. I am going to say this one last time, at the age of four my mother's husband tried to rape me; it must never be an "It depends." It's ALWAYS a "Yes" with your mouth and "It depends" in your head.

Honestly, there really should be no need for me to use my own story to get this point across but in 99% of my presentations I have had to use my story because

I wanted every participant to leave uttering a "Yes" with their mouth and "It depends" in their head. That is my desire for you too, that by the time you've finished reading this book you will have no doubt in your mind that if you are ever asked the question, "Can you keep a secret?", you will unequivocally respond "Yes" with your mouth and "It depends" in your head.

My Journey Into Public Speaking

◆

I am going to start in the middle of my story since my life journey cannot be complete until the day I am dead and buried, which I am hoping is a long way away. I hope that doesn't sound too morbid, but I have yet to accomplish the things that many people of my age have had for close to a decade. As I have often put it, "I'm not young; I'm old. I have no job, no husband, and no house. I'm a gypsy or homeless person, or whatever else you want to call me."

Is that really the way I define myself? No, it isn't, that is just the way I have been described by some 'wonderful' individuals who had nothing better to do than to judge and criticize the way I lived my life instead of providing a practical and realistic alternative. Telling me to get a paid lawyer's job had been exactly that, impractical and unrealistic, because there was no magic to U.S. laws of immigration. The same rules would have applied whether I was a farmer, teacher or lawyer. First and foremost, I am an immigrant requiring work authorization, citizenship, or a Green card.

I have now reached a point in my life where I shy away from what the church calls, 'wise counsel,'[4] because the only 'wisdom' I have received, thus far, was to stop obeying God. Now those wise counsellors, who usually held some form of leadership position as an elder or pastor, never actually came outright and said that. Instead, they spoke with a great deal of authority, notably with the absence of God in the room, because not once did those meetings ever begin with a prayer to invite Him in.

A lot of people entered my life halfway through the current journey I was on and, therefore, did not understand the foundation that had been previously built. One such person told me that I should not get excited by the luxury and that I needed to fast and pray. Considering the countless years I had spent moving between houses, sleeping on the floor, showering with a cold bucket of water, and residing in filthy conditions, I believed that I was fully entitled to enjoy the luxury. It lasted one and a half weeks, to be exact, and I thoroughly appreciated the experience of living in a 'palace' complete with swimming pool, despite the fact that I never took the opportunity to go swimming.

I am blessed, which is something I would never deny; in fact, in my opinion if God had favorites, I am certainly one of them. He has blessed me so abundantly with amazing experiences; travelling throughout the world

---

4   *"The way of a fool [is] right in his own eyes: but he that hearkeneth unto counsel [is] wise."* Proverbs 12:15 (KJV)

with little or no money. It is only because of His grace and covering that I have not been raped, robbed or murdered and I have complete confidence in the God that I serve that this would never happen. Why? For a number of reasons:

1. People have been actively waiting on the sidelines for one or all of the above to happen just so they could shout out, "You see, Juanita wasn't listening to God after all. She was taking all these unnecessary risks, putting her life in danger. I told you so."

2. I have been living in obedience to God, and, therefore, when He has called me, figuratively speaking, to the lions' den[5] or fiery furnace,[6] I am in the safest place that I could be, because I am in His will.

When I am in God's will, the lions are on a hunger strike and the fire doesn't burn. I, therefore, do not believe that I owe anyone an explanation for how I live my life, but I have always been intentional in telling people that "If I wasn't obedient to God then I would be married and living in sin." "Why in sin? Marriage isn't sin." Someone once asked me so I explained, "There is a Muslim man that I could marry right now; THAT would be a sin according to the Bible, and not my personal opinion,

---

[5] *"My God hath sent his angel, and hath shut the lions' mouths, that they have not hurt me."* Daniel 6:22 (KJV)

[6] Daniel 3 (KJV)

because I'd be unequally yoked with an unbeliever"[7] and doing what I wanted which would be the exact opposite of what I am currently doing. Instead, I have been doing what God wanted, because He is far more stubborn than I am and, although I haven't exactly been enjoying my life, generally speaking, I wouldn't have it any other way ... well aside from wanting the husband of course, sooner, rather than later.

A lot of people envied me and my life without knowing any of the challenges that I experienced on an almost daily basis. They saw all of my smiling pictures and noted the numerous travel stops each year, but despite having travelled to twenty-nine countries thus far, it was not as much fun as people have often perceived. My photos were grossly misleading because they were posed, thus not accurately reflecting the reality of my situation. My finances were minimal, therefore, there were many things that I missed out on, from exploring the beautiful country and its beaches, to trying the vegan versions of the infamous local meat dishes; and although I frequently country hopped, I was often dusting off my feet at various homes.[8]

I think I'm getting ahead of myself, so let me start in the middle of my story with Trinidad and Tobago.

People would often ask me, "Why Trinidad?" or "Do you like Trinidad?" to which I'd reply, "I didn't choose

---

[7] *"Be ye not unequally yoked together with unbelievers:"* 2 Corinthians 6:14 (KJV)

[8] *"And whosoever shall not receive you, nor hear your words, when ye depart out of that house or city, shake off the dust of your feet."* Matthew 10:14 (KJV)

Trinidad and Tobago; God literally brought me here all expenses paid to a five-star hotel for a judges' conference." With regards to me liking or disliking the islands, my response has usually been, "I don't like it here because it's not safe. Without transport or a companion, I cannot leave my home. But I love speaking here on human trafficking."

Now, let's start a little farther back than Trinidad and Tobago and allow the journey to begin four years earlier when after two failed attempts sitting for the New York Bar exam, by the grace of God, I finally passed.

Now you may have noticed my frequent references to God and probably when you first picked up this book, you had anticipated the pages to be filled with factual information, including a horrific story or two thrown in on the issue of human trafficking and sexual abuse. You were not mistaken; that information is contained here, however, I deem it appropriate to create a foundation by introducing myself, my story, and the journey that brought me to the point of writing this book.

I can make no apologies for my conversations about God because if it wasn't for God this book would never have been written, let alone published. Therefore, I want you to know which God I serve whilst also avoiding any confusion concerning my motivations in life. My desire is for you to be inspired by my story and the gift of faith that I have and to see the hand of God in my life, whether you believe in His existence or not. Simply put, my story is really unbelievable, so much so, that it cannot be contained here in this one book.

This God that I have been continually referring to has a son called Jesus Christ, who is described in the King James Version of the Holy Bible. I have intentionally placed emphasis here on the version of the Bible I am referring to, because since 2012 Amazon has made the Queen James Bible[9] available for purchase by those who lead or believe that leading a homosexual lifestyle is not a sin. I have not read nor do I endorse such a Bible.

In this day and age, as there are many gods and many lords, there is a need for me to give further clarification. My denomination of Christianity is irrelevant here because depending upon where you are in the world you may have a perception of my denomination that would be grossly inaccurate.

Suffice it to say, I am a born-again Christian, which goes some way to distinguish me from a number of denominations that do not use such terminology. As a little girl once asked me, "What does that mean?" My way of describing being born-again, is being 'drowned' in a swimming pool and then being lifted back up again out of the water. Similar to the story of Jesus' baptism at the River Jordan, where he was placed under the water, then brought up again; a dove came down from heaven and the Lord spoke.[10] I am disappointed to say that there was no dove, parting of clouds, or a voice from heaven during my baptism, since it was indoors,

---

9   Amazon. "The Queens James Bible", Accessed August 28, 2018. https:// www. amazon.com/The-Queen-James-Bible/dp/0615724531

10   Matthew 3:13-17 (KJV)

but I feel confident in saying that the Lord was well pleased.[11]

My faith is in Jesus Christ, the Holy Spirit and the living God from the Holy Bible. I read the King James Version of the Bible and believe EVERYTHING that has been written in that book. Suffice to say I am not a pick and mix Christian but I believe in the entire Bible, both Old and New Testament. The Bible is not my guideline, instead it is the manual of my life because God created me and thus knows His creation best. Therefore, when I refer to God, I am referring to God from the Holy Bible who came to Earth as a baby,[12] the child of a virgin,[13] who died and rose again on the third day.[14] I do not focus on Mary or the Saints. My focus is primarily on Jesus Christ, the Holy Spirit and God the Father.

This faith I have in an unseen God has been the driving force behind the way I have lived my life, and as I have frequently said, "No person in their right mind would volunteer six years unpaid unless they were crazy or they were motivated by someone or something." I am not crazy, but if I were, crazy for Jesus would be an accurate description.

On the contrary, most people called me brave which was one of my two pet peeves. The other one was when

---

[11] *"And lo a voice from heaven, saying, This is my beloved Son, in whom I am well pleased."* Matthew 3:17 (KJV)

[12] Matthew 2 (KJV)

[13] *"[S]he was found with child of the Holy Ghost."* Matthew 1:18 (KJV)

[14] John 19 (KJV); Luke 24 (KJV)

people misspelled my surname. Since my first name is 'unique' in many parts of the world I am used to it being misspelled, mispronounced and even instructed on how it should be spelt and said; but my surname is really easy, so easy in fact that the second e was usually omitted so I frequently had to educate people that it was "Headley not Head-ly".

The brave thing, however, irritated me immensely. Why? Because it simply isn't true! In my opinion, the bravest guy in the Bible was Jonah because he disobeyed God.[15] I am nothing like Jonah, but I liken myself more to Joseph,[16] which unbeknownst to many was the first recorded human trafficking story in the Bible.

I have experienced betrayal by my family and betrayal by my employers; In June 2021 I was, thrown in a St. Vincent jail, and am figuratively speaking waiting for the keys to get out so that I can experience the victory that concluded Joseph's story.[17]

Instead of mislabeling me as brave, I should be called obedient. Would that be because I have been obedient 100% of the time? No, of course not, but obedience was why I have been living my life in such an incredibly unconventional way. God has always spoken directly to me, but please understand it is not an audible voice

---

[15] Jonah 1 (KJV)

[16] Genesis 37; 39 (KJV)

[17] Genesis 41:41-43 (KJV); Check out the additional chapter at the back of this book: "6 Strategies to Surviving Jail Time", and sign up to my mailing list on www.changingcases.org be the first to hear about the release of my new book: "Attorney Behind Bars".

from the sky. The simplest way to explain what I mean is that a thought would appear in my mind which would be followed by external occurrences confirming that thought. One such instance occurred in October 2015 when I was mentally planning which country I would visit during the summer. In my mind's eye India popped up but I wasn't sure. My lack of certainty prevented me from disclosing to anyone that this was indeed my plan, instead it was nothing more than a mere idea.

I asked God for confirmation and received it in the following ways:

1. Due to power failure on the train lines I arrived at church five minutes before the service concluded. I was obviously late, however, I arrived just in time to hear a missionary talk about her experience in India;

2. On Easter Sunday when the sermon would always be focused on Jesus death and resurrection, the pastor mentioned for two to three minutes his experiences in India;

3. A documentary screening on human trafficking in India was taking place in New York. I could not afford the ticket, so I prayed to God that if He indeed wanted me to go to India He would provide me free admission to the event. On the day of the film showing an e-mail went around at 'work' offering free tickets. When I sat in the auditorium that evening I was fully immersed in the film because it was the first time I was

watching real life footage of the country I would be going to in just a few months.

4. A few days before leaving the U.S. for India I was at a church concert where they showed the trailer of a movie called 'SOLD' and then shared that they were building a home called 'Hope House' in India, just like in the film.

That is just one example, but I have found that throughout my life God would speak to me through signs and confirmations which were often visible enough for the people around me to see them too.

A more simplistic way of describing my relationship with God would be that we are on the same frequency, so for example if God was an AT&T phone subscriber, I too was on AT&T.

The sad reality is that there are many Christians who are not hearing or experiencing God in their lives because they are a "Verizon phone subscriber" whilst God subscribes to AT&T. This is figuratively speaking of course as I am in no way promoting AT&T as a means to communicate with God, it is just merely an example that I use with the phone subscriber changing depending upon which part of the world I am located.

Although my Christian walk began when I was sixteen, I have travelled a particularly adventurous journey with God over the last six years where He has proved Himself faithful time and time again.

I have met hundreds of Christians from all over the world and in my opinion one of the biggest hindrances in their walk with Christ was their lack of faith. Sadly, I have often felt as though the church is full of hypocrisy with so many Christians professing Christ with their mouth but not their actions.

The Bible says, "By their fruit you will know them."[18] This scripture can be likened to a fruit tree in England. During the winter season, the leaves fall off and the tree becomes barren. By looking at it, the casual observer would have no idea of the type of fruit that tree would produce. The individual may hazard a guess that it could be an apple or pear tree but until it bears fruit there would be no way to determine exactly which type of tree it is.

Another scripture that would be appropriate here is, *"For out of the abundance of the heart the mouth speaketh."*[19] This means that whatever a person is thinking and feeling in their heart would be evidenced from the things that they say. I believe this is something that even non believers would agree with. When a person feels happy and loved it is reflected in the positive and affirming words that they speak. Whereas, when a person has feelings of anger, or is filled with bitterness and rage their tone and words would typically be harsh, aggressive, and possibly even abusive in nature.

An experience I had with a pastor should give you better context. It was my first time meeting her despite

---

[18] *"Ye shall know them by their fruits."* Matthew 7:16 (KJV)

[19] Matthew 12:34 (KJV)

us communicating via WhatsApp during the past five months. As our written conversation had been primarily surface, I didn't know what to expect during our first interaction.

The first question she asked me was where I lived and if I paid rent? It was an odd question in my opinion because I wondered why my finances were an appropriate topic of conversation. I rather assertively explained that as I was an unpaid lawyer I did not pay rent but lived with friends of friends. Her immediate reaction was, "That's dangerous."

I of course wholeheartedly disagreed, and proceeded to defend my case by explaining, "Walking on water,[20] hanging out in the lion's den, standing in the fiery furnace; and talking to a burning bush[21] were all dangerous, but when you were in God's will those were the safest places to be."

The pastor then explained her personal experiences of hosting missionaries for free for years, and how some of those individuals took advantage of what was given to them, repaying the generous hospitality with dishonesty and theft. Now, that was the pastor's experience. I however, unlike her guests am not a missionary. On the contrary, I am merely a public speaker and anti-human trafficking advocate who also happens to be Christian.

---

[20] Matthew 14:22-29 (KJV)

[21] Exodus 3:1-15 (KJV)

Anyone who knows me could defend my actions in a court of law as being wholly focused on speaking engagements - not socializing or going to the beach. The only thing I truly desire is a quiet place to sleep, nothing more or less. The internet is always a luxury but not a necessity (depending upon where I am in the world) and the facility of a fridge and microwave are always appreciated.

Over the last six years I've been accommodated by friends of friends and not one hair on my head has ever been disturbed. Spiritually speaking there has been absolutely no danger in how I live my life because wherever I was I had been sent there by God. Culturally, I believe that many people in Trinidad and Tobago live in fear and paranoia. People would frequently tell me to be careful to which my response was, "I don't do careful, because that requires me to take care of myself. Instead I allow God to protect me."

Again, coming back to those references I made earlier, "The lion's den, fiery furnace, and walking on water;" if those Bible characters who were the 'stars' of those stories were careful they would not have been in any of those positions which were all dangerous with seemingly life-threatening consequences.

Through meeting many modern-day Christians, I have been led to believe that when Peter was walking on water,[22] the other disciples inside the boat were telling

---

[22] *"Then Peter got down out of the boat, walked on the water and came toward Jesus."* Matthew 14:29 (KJV)

him to get back in. When Daniel was in the lion's den, I believe there were people already preparing for his funeral, and when Shadrach, Meshach, and Abednego got into the fiery furnace, I believe the bystanders were holding their noses in anticipation of the stench of three burning bodies.

The Bible says, *"Now faith is the substance of things hoped for, the evidence of things not seen."*[23] An example of faith would be having insufficient money in the bank but believing that you would have all the necessary funds for that expensive flight ticket with an impending departure date. The evidence of faith would not be using MasterCard, getting a loan or borrowing money from friends, but instead trusting that an invisible God would provide you with that visible flight ticket.

My understanding of the lack of faith demonstrated by many Christians and pastors was that they lived in a place of provision. They were employed, had financial stability, and were surrounded by supportive friends and family. In other words, they had safety nets just in case things didn't go as planned. Consequently, if they suddenly encountered a situation of dire need they would simply pull out their credit card or borrow from someone; in other words, God became their last resort instead of their first solution.

In my opinion, in countries like India, South America and Africa, where there are people living far below

---

[23] Hebrews 11:1 (KJV)

the poverty line in complete destitution and poverty, they experience the hand of God so much more than the average Westerner because all they have is prayer. When there is no money, food or provision they would pray and experience the supernatural become the natural.

In my own life I have also experienced the supernatural consistently, so much so that when people shared with me their praise report or testimony I would occasionally respond with silence and a blank stare. Why? I already knew how their story would end and was not surprised or wowed by what they shared. Having consistently experienced 'wow' moments in my life, I wouldn't always show my excitement on the outside, but I was always excited on the inside. In fact, every praise report that I heard further strengthened my faith and belief that God is real.

He has been real in my world and I believe He is also real in the life of many of my friends despite them not all being Christian. One particular friend that I have known for six years has been privy to my journey as and when it transpired. Comparing the past six years to a roller-coaster would be a serious understatement and would never do my experiences true justice.

There have been so many instances when I would message that friend saying, "What will I eat tomorrow, where will I sleep?"[24] Her response would always be

---

[24] *"Therefore take no thought, saying, What shall we eat? Or, What shall we drink?"* Matthew 6:31 (NIV)

the same, "Your God will provide," and do you know what? She has always been right. I have never spent a night sleeping on the street and never unintentionally skipped a meal. My God has always provided just as the scripture promises, *"Yet have I not seen the righteous forsaken, nor his seed begging bread."*[25]

My friend's words rang true to the point that I got annoyed hearing them, I wanted her to feel sorry for me but instead her words were a constant reminder of God's faithfulness to me in the past. In the end, I actually stopped sharing with her my plights because I could already predict her response, and although she didn't know it, it was very much a Matthew 6:25 situation.[26] My God has provided and would continue to provide, great is His faithfulness (which is actually the first line of a famous hymn and also my favorite song). Anyway, I've digressed; I just want to lay a foundation down about who I am and the God that I serve.

As I shared earlier I finally passed my exams and was sworn in as a New York attorney in June 2014. It was my third attempt at an exam that I had prepared for from across the pond in England. I have never been educated in America and I was not particularly studious while preparing for the Bar exam hence why I had previously failed.

---

[25] Psalm 37:25 (KJV)

[26] Matthew 6:25-34 (KJV)

On my second retake, although I was a mere sixteen marks away from passing I was ready to call it quits. I lacked the motivation to re-sit the exam a third time especially as the July exam was easier than the February exam, and it had a higher passing mark.

In 2014 my mum heavily encouraged me to take the February exam which I had been adamantly against. I had absolutely no interest in sitting for the Bar exam again, especially bearing in mind that it was deemed harder than the ones I had failed previously. Begrudgingly, I prepared for the exam like never before. I had a direct conversation with God, and I told Him, "If I do not pass my exams I'll become a missionary."

To my utter surprise and amazement, I passed the Bar exam, but I considered myself something of a self - made missionary.

Since I have not been sent around the world by a church, I could not be considered your typical missionary, therefore I would simply tell people that I had been sent by Jesus.

The way I had lived in the U.S. was certainly not what I had envisioned. When I had initially decided to take the New York Bar exam, it was with the intention of eventually becoming a California lawyer. However, after taking the second hardest Bar exam three times I no longer had any interest in taking what was titled the first hardest Bar exam in the entire country.

I hated New York but nonetheless decided to try my luck at acquiring gainful employment and sponsorship. Unfortunately, my efforts proved unfruitful so in 2015 I flew back to England for a paralegal position in a boutique law firm located a stone's throw away from my home. After two years of being in the U.S. with border crossings every six months I was finally returning home.

A few months before I returned home I had been in contact with a lawyer through the social media site LinkedIn. He had invited me to be a guest on his radio show for a discussion on English law. Back in 2011 I had graduated from Teesside University, but since we were in 2015 I did not remember anything about English law.

This was, however, a great opportunity for me so I jumped at the chance to be on air. I am using the word jumped but crawled would be a more accurate description. Despite how studious and proactive I had been at university, something had changed. I procrastinated and delayed my radio appearance because I knew 'nothing' about English law.

When I was offered the job in England I had to make a mad dash to the recording studio to prevent losing that opportunity. Since it was in Nassau County I travelled to the station on the Long Island Rail Road. It was my first time using that mode of transportation and because of my confusion I almost missed my train. Instead, in running for the train I tripped and damaged the heel of my shoe. Fortunately, I had just enough time to salvage my heel before the train departed.

That crisis averted, I settled comfortably into my seat taking frequent stock of the passing stations. The host who I had never met before was waiting for me at the train station. We got into his car and drove a short distance to the studio. I would never have known it at the time, but this fellow attorney was to become the one consistency in my life; sending me job advertisements, offering unsolicited but well-meaning advice and providing me with much needed support.

This was my first media appearance and although it was a pre-recorded interview I'd been informed that it would not be edited unless I cursed, and since I do not use expletives there would clearly be no opportunity for a cut. Despite that I was so nervous that my hands actually sweat so much that they left a circular wet patch on my dress where they had been resting on my lap.

Thankfully, my nerves did not get the better of me and the show went really well, irrespective of how unprepared I was. At the time, the studio desk had been covered with dozens of papers filled with answers to potential questions, however, I was unable to move any of them because the rustling would have been heard over the air.

That night when I returned home I listened to the show with my housemate. I was amazed! The recording sounded fantastic! I really could not believe it.

When my best friend heard the recording, she commented on how professional I sounded when responding to each question. I told her that I actually had no idea what the answer was but was trying to make myself sound knowledgeable. Unbeknownst to me at that time, my first radio interview was only the start of many media appearances to come on a much wider international scale.

In 2016 I made multiple appearances on the radio program, 'Law You Should Know,' including as co-host. However, unlike that first memorable recording, my hands no longer left sweat marks on my clothes, but I remained nervous despite knowing that the interviews were always pre-recorded.

In March 2016 I had the privilege of organizing a human trafficking panel discussion at the Queens County Bar Association (QCBA). I invited two panelists to share their expertise on the subject with the ultimate goal of forming a professional relationship with them, which I hoped would materialize into paid employment.

As I had been previously encouraged by a New York judge I contacted QCBA and requested that I be acknowledged on the event flier as the program organizer. To my utter dismay the flier had me incorrectly listed as a speaker on human trafficking. I was beyond distraught! I kicked and screamed when I saw the QCBA's mistake, and I distinctly remember telling my mum that I could not speak on human trafficking because I did not know anything about the topic.

Thankfully the organizers were gracious enough to allow me to introduce the panelists thus giving me a platform to speak-albeit not on human trafficking as the flier had indicated.

In my opinion I had performed terribly, reading in a monotonous tone straight from the bios, and although I had tried to memorize the credentials of the panelists I failed miserably. I was glad when it was finally over. It had been a failed first attempt at public speaking as a lawyer, but it was definitely a learning experience.

That experience and the entire incident requires a great deal of emphasis here because I believe that it was unequivocally prophetic as well as God's way of preparing me for the future.

Notably, in hind sight and seemingly disconnected from everything else that was going on at the time, it was another element of preparation that occurred two months earlier when I implemented the advice of a fellow attorney who encouraged me to never be perturbed by a cost but to always ask for a scholarship. This was the best advice I have ever received and is very much Biblical as evidenced by the scripture *"Ask, and it shall be given you."*[27]

Asking paid off because I received a $1000.00 scholarship for Decker's Communication course. It is embarrassing to say that I actually knew nothing about the program but went along anyway to what turned out to be a life transforming two days. The course taught me absolutely everything I needed to

---

[27] Matthew 7:7 (KJV)

know about communication and laid the foundation for every future speaking engagement I would have from that day forward. Subsequently, in a bid to implement what I had learned I would jump at every opportunity I got to demonstrate my Decker training during prayer meetings, seminars or conferences. I inadvertently became incredibly self-critical and would often mentally beat myself up for not gesticulating, making eye contact or moving around.

When I spoke at my belated birthday party in September of that year my notes contained only a handful of bullet points. With minimal written information I entertained my audience who laughed, smiled and were thoroughly enraptured by my stories. The following day when (again with only the use of bullet points) I shared my testimony at church, which was something I had been doing for the past decade, someone came up to me after the service and said it was the best testimony I had ever given. Those words of affirmation spoke volumes to me; the Decker training had finally paid off, I was comfortable with my bullet points and the audience remained engaged with my new method of communicating.

After all the years of scripted testimonies when my hands would be sweating and my legs and voice would be shaking, somehow miraculously I had developed the confidence to speak to a room full of people without verbatim notes, whilst even making and sustaining eye contact. To say that I had come a long way was truly an understatement.

My Journey Into Public Speaking

As I like to put it, I was trained by the best. Unbeknownst to the average layman, criminal lawyers in the U.S. tend to go to acting school and are therefore generally speaking into theatrics; they wave around weapons, bang the table and entertain the jury. As terrible as this sounds I really want to be a criminal lawyer so I too can get my day in court.

In my opinion, absolutely everything in the U.S. is either big or loud, thus whenever I would present, that was exactly what I demonstrated, big and loud actions.

After having spent five months volunteering in India and then celebrating my belated birthday in England I returned to the U.S. Unlike the four previous years, this time God relocated me to Washington D.C. where I began volunteering for NCOSE – the National Center on Sexual Exploitation.

When I first arrived, I was staying in a hostel before taking all of my possessions with me to Texas, where in the spirit of 'luxury' I was flown over for NCOSEs annual summit. It was my first time being flown anywhere all expenses paid, which was going to become something of a trend over the next few years.

The conference was amazing. I learnt so much (especially about exploitation in the pornography industry) and made some great connections. Unfortunately, the position was to be short-lived and by the beginning of November I was 'jobless.' It all happened so suddenly and was not what I would have anticipated but it was all part of God's plan.

This plan concerned a film called 'SOLD' which had become a recent project of mine. It was Hollywood's depiction of child trafficking and prostitution, taking viewers on a journey that began with deceit when the main character 'Lakshimi' was taken from her home in Nepal to Mumbai to pursue the promise of a job.

I had heard about the film prior to my trip to India and upon my return to the U.S. I was very interested in watching it. A screening had just taken place outside of D.C. However, had I known about it earlier I could not have attended because I was unable to afford the $20.00 ticket. As ridiculous as this sounds, I made the decision right then and there that since I could not afford to pay $20.00 to watch the film, I would screen it myself, so I could watch it for free.

Shortly thereafter I did get the opportunity to watch the film for free where one of the audience members was so deeply impacted that she kept gasping at all the uncomfortable scenes. It was a huge distraction for the rest of us in the room including one individual who was actually a survivor of sexual exploitation.

Aside from that, I was really excited to finally have the opportunity to watch 'SOLD.' At the end of the evening I stuck around to network with the small number of other attendees and more importantly the host. She had been doing amazing work fighting human trafficking in the D.C. area and I wanted to volunteer at her organization.

We talked briefly and I shared with her that I would be hosting my own screening of 'SOLD.' This was because despite the fact that I had just seen the movie for free, my project was far from over. In fact, I saw that viewing as my opportunity to get a sneak preview ahead of my big event.

Through my research I discovered that a license had to be paid prior to showing the film. The cost attached to this license was $800.00, an amount I could not have in any way afforded. I discussed this with the evening's host at length and was reassured that she would take care of it or words to that effect.

That night when I left the screening I had the clear understanding that the film license would be paid for, therefore all I needed to do was organize a venue and panelists. Unbeknownst to me there was actually no agreement to pay for the license and I was subsequently left feeling deceived. When I later spoke with the host she claimed her understanding was that I would pay for the license; this needless to say was a complete lie, further solidified by the fact that she had given me cash to pay for a cab ride home. I subsequently decided to separate myself from her and work on my project without her assistance or involvement.

A short while later I attended a human trafficking program at a church that was centrally located in D.C. The room did not have the aesthetics I was looking for, but I'd been informed that there was a larger church auditorium downstairs. I was interested in using this venue for my event because of its locality, but deep in my heart I did not want the screening to be held at a church.

Irrespective of that feeling I contacted the church immediately to request the space for my event. The communication was slow which left me feeling frustrated. Time was running out because I wanted to obtain a venue two weeks before Christmas to enable me to begin sending out invitations.

After my last program at QCBA with its really poor turnout I knew a lot of work had to be done to ensure that did not happen again. When discussing this with another young lawyer he told me that I needed to make people feel as though I was personally inviting them; they needed to feel special, which an e-mail or WhatsApp message would not accomplish.

First things first: I began e-mailing all the NGOs in the entire United States, inviting the CEOs and founders to be a part of my panel. There was indeed an overwhelmingly positive response, but the caveat was the frequent request for flights and accommodation, something which I could not even afford for myself.

Everything I did was strategic. It wasn't that I had nothing better to do with my time but I was casting my net wide and implementing the advice given by a N.Y. Judge, "Organize a panel event and invite participants who you'd like to hire you."

In addition to those invitations I would also request permission to use the logos of the organizations on my program brochure to show solidarity and support and that they were 'sponsoring' the event, albeit in name only. It certainly worked because I would occasionally get suggestions from people that I should ask my sponsors to do various things, advice which I promptly discarded. Things moved along very slowly with about four 'sponsors.' In the early planning stages a lot of my time was spent designing the flier especially whenever new 'sponsors' would appear.

Acquiring panelists was easy enough despite how slow the process of confirmation took. Things were beginning to take shape despite the absence of a venue and the $800.00 license fee. The church that I had wanted to use had been dragging their heels. I had been praying about it consistently and sending regular correspondence to the church but to no avail. When they finally got around to making a decision they said that the room I had requested could not accommodate the capacity I had chosen. I was frustrated because after all the weeks of delay I didn't understand why they hadn't told me that immediately.

I foolishly decided to place a new request complying with their capacity requirement only to eventually get a response saying that the room was not available on that day. I felt like a child's toy that was being begrudgingly played with. Although I did not want my event to be held in a church environment I was greatly irritated by the unnecessary delays and lack of straightforward and concise information.

I now had no choice but to cast my net wider by reaching out to people I knew, and also contacting the management of venues I'd been in. Whilst experiencing all of these challenges I was still trying to acquire the $800.00 license fee. An acquaintance gave me the number of a guy and encouraged me to contact him. He was an ex-convict who had been released from jail deemed an innocent man. I had actually met him at a conference where he had been very insistent that we go out and have drinks. I was in no way interested in having any drinks with him, so I'd made my excuses.

I was told that he would be very supportive of what I was doing and that it was highly likely he'd give me the money for the license. How wrong my acquaintance had been! So wrong that I'd had to suffer through over an hour of negativity being told that I should not show a film on India and that it was the voice of God speaking through him instructing me to focus on my Filipino orphanage. After that conversation he would send me the odd flirtatious text until I eventually blocked him.

Whilst looking for panelists I was also looking for a co-host. The individual who had originally agreed to the position had proven to be completely useless, over-promising and under-delivering. Fortunately, I established a professional relationship with someone in the anti-trafficking world who agreed to co-host and was indeed a tremendous help. The date I had originally chosen was Thursday, January 26th however he was unavailable, so I moved the event forward to Wednesday, January 25th.

A venue that I had contacted previously had agreed to provide me the space, free of charge if I could provide information establishing that I was a registered nonprofit. My co-host was part of a nonprofit organization, so he would have been able to furnish the necessary documentation. Unfortunately, that venue also fell through.

Mid December was fast approaching, and I still had no venue. My panel was coming together, so well in fact that I had far too many panelists! I also had plenty of 'sponsors.' Being really slim on options I signed up for venue space at the library. The last time I had been returning books I'd had the opportunity to view some of the rooms downstairs and also speak with a supervisor. She did in fact explain to me that it was too late for the library to advertise my event or provide me with a PA system, but I could certainly make a request for the room.

This was one of those situations where I felt, "If only I had known sooner." In fact, I would have if I hadn't heeded to the advice of my landlord. She had told me that the library would not allow movie screenings unless the movie was from the library's collection. That may have previously been fact and her reality; however, my God's reality could always supersede the laws, rules and reality of the world. The lesson I learned from that experience was the continual application of the scripture, *"Ask, and it shall be given you."*[28]

I still trusted Him for a miracle however, so although I was not within the required time frame, I made my request known and submitted an application for the necessary assistance and AV equipment. Unfortunately,

---

[28] *Ibid.*

my request was denied. I had also made a request for the event space downstairs and was expecting a response within the standard three days. Within three hours of sending my e-mail I received a response confirming I had the space.

It was a miracle! I finally had a free venue. This meant that I could now begin inviting people to the event.

Whilst all this was going on I had been in contact with a friend. My plan was to visit and spend some time with her during her college winter break. We had gone back and forth discussing the arrangements but to no avail. In the end I decided not to visit her but still travel to the West Coast. My plan had been to spend a day in Seattle before travelling to California and visiting some of the local anti- trafficking NGOs.

Less than 24-hours after booking my flight, I received an e-mail about a 'SOLD' screening being held in Hollywood. I do not believe in coincidences, but the event was 'coincidentally' during the week when I would be in Southern California. I thought to myself if that wasn't a sign from God then I didn't know what was.

I then posted on my Facebook wall that I would be attending the event. A short while later I saw that my post had received a like, from the Hollywood actor, David Arquette. I was astounded! I then sent him FB and Twitter messages inviting him to my screenings. They remained unanswered but that didn't stop me from praying.

As my search for a New York venue continued, I reached out to some fellow attorneys from the Christian Lawyer's Society. One of those attorneys worked at Google and had been trying to secure me a New York venue so that I could screen the film both there and in D.C. Unfortunately, the New York location was unavailable but the D.C. Google office was. Despite already having my D.C. event organized I decided to take advantage of this opportunity and hold a screening at Google too.

The plan was to have the first event in the library then the following day at Google. When I explained this to my co- host he was confused and didn't see the point or need to do two screenings. I told him that by having these events back to back, people who couldn't attend on one day could come to the other and also share with friends.

A short while after I received an e-mail that 'Bronxworks' in New York had approved my request to hold a 'SOLD' screening on Friday.

This was nothing short of a miracle, from not having a venue to securing not one, not two, but three venues in two States over three days. A miracle was an understatement because I now had a mammoth task ahead of me; notwithstanding the cost of three licenses.

Now unbeknownst to me the license was not actually $800.00 as there was a sliding scale depending on a number of factors. A friend of a friend, who I had yet to meet in person, had written me a check of $350.00 towards the cost of my first license. As had been customary I again revisited the 'Tugg' website, however this time with a more exploratory nature. I then discovered that with a reduced number of seats and free admission to the film there was a license available for $350.00. I was astonished! All this time I had been trying to solicit individuals to pay $800.00 for a license when a considerably cheaper option was available.

That for me was a clear sign from God, *"This is the way, walk ye in it."*[29] What was quite amusing about the whole thing was that I don't watch T.V. let alone movies, but here I was screening a film three times.

My license could now be paid. I had three venues in place, panel speakers and 'sponsors,' and as the time drew near I began sending out customary e-mails inviting people to my events. However, after my experience at QCBA I knew that e-mails would simply not be enough, let alone WhatsApp messages.

The week before my event I found myself in Northern and Southern California. It was my first trip back in seven years and I was looking forward to a swim in the sea. I had no such luck since it was January and although the sun was shining the weather was misleading. Instead, I used the time to telephone everyone I knew in New York and Washington D.C. and personally invite them to my screenings. It was incredibly time consuming, even more so when the call was answered. However, I had been strategic in the

---

[29] Isaiah 30:21 (KJV)

timing of my interaction because I made the calls on a public holiday when almost everyone was at home from work.

During my time in Southern California little did I know at the time of purchasing my flights, that there would be a Hollywood screening of 'SOLD.' I could hardly believe my luck and timing and was thoroughly excited about meeting the stars who I wanted to attend my events.

The day finally arrived, and I was dressed for the red carpet. It was an amazing night where I met the main character 'Lakshimi,' actress Seirah Royin, Producer Jane Charles, Academy Award winning director Jeffrey Brown, and actor David Arquette, not to mention just a few weeks earlier I had been on the phone with 'SOLD' author Patricia McCormick.

As the night drew to a close I made a decision to intercept David Arquette on his way out of the movie theater to solicit his attendance at my events. I strategically positioned myself on the steps at the front left-hand side of the movie theatre and as soon as he began to make his exit I ran alongside him sharing quick fire who I was and my intentions. I suspect he had no idea who I was despite the fact that he had liked my post on Facebook following which I had taken the initiative to message him multiple times on both Facebook and Twitter. I told him that I was screening the movie around the world and would love his attendance in New York and Washington D.C.

I'm not sure what caught his attention, but he actually stopped walking and listened to me. I gave him my business card and managed to get a couple of pictures together before he left. Less than fifteen minutes later I received an e-mail from him with his cell phone number. I was dumbfounded. I could never have foreseen that in my wildest dreams. I had, in my possession, the personal cell phone number of David Arquette!

The next day I e-mailed everyone I knew and told them about my experience and how I now had David on speed dial. For the first time in my life my inbox was full. In 24-hours I received over a hundred e-mails from people who wanted a piece of the action. What they didn't know was that I had absolutely no intention of soliciting David for their campaigns because I needed to protect my relationship with him. A few days later I was back in Washington D.C., just 24-hours ahead of my 'tour' of three 'SOLD' screenings in three states, over three days.

Finally, all my hard work and efforts had paid off following the tireless preparation over the preceding months when I had been going to bed at 2 a.m. and waking up at 4 a.m. or 5 a.m. It therefore came as no surprise when I developed shingles, which I mistakenly assumed were bed bugs thus suffered in silence, knowing that I could not afford the medical bills.

Fortunately, there had been a medical doctor at the 'JUST' conference giving a human trafficking presentation. Not only did I uncover the reality that survivors of sexual abuse sometimes have a lot of anger, but she also diagnosed my bout of shingles and wrote me a prescription all free of charge. If that wasn't enough good fortune the pharmacist redeemed a coupon that she had, which significantly reduced the cost of my medication by over $100.00 and less than a fortnight later I had made a full recovery.

Being in good spirits I was certainly looking forward to the first of my three screenings, an event which was to exceed the expectations of everyone involved and become a tremendous success. I had no doubt in my mind that the God I serve would come through for me just as He'd done so consistently in the past.

Day one fell on Wednesday, January 25th, 2017, at the Martin Luther King Jr. Memorial Library in Washington D.C. There was so much preparation for me to do to ensure that everything ran smoothly and of course the event was not without its challenges.

Due to budget limitations I was unable to afford a PA system, consequently my co-host opted to bring along a pair of laptop speakers to enable the film audio to be heard throughout the room. This was a bigger blessing in disguise than we would have originally known because less than an hour and a half before the screening was due to begin I got the call I'd been waiting for. Someone had kindly donated money to hire a PA system. In a mad dash across town, some of my volunteers collected the equipment and brought it back to the library all in the nick of time.

This was a miracle, but the problem was, since no one knew how to set up the equipment they made the false assumption that some parts were missing. In the end we couldn't use it, but instead the panelists were required simply to project their voices. This was not a major setback due to the layout and acoustics of the room. The much bigger issue was that my laptop did not have a HDMI port to enable it to be utilized for the SKYPE conversation with David Arquette.

This was a problem since tickets had been advertised with reference to an appearance by David Arquette (of course without mentioning the fact that it would be via webcam). To pull this off we needed an Apple Mac which neither my host nor I had. I did the only thing I could under the circumstances and that was to use my initiative and ask the audience. Fortunately a fellow attorney saved the day because he had his MacBook in his car.

Finally, with everything in place we were officially able to begin. The room was packed one hundred and fifty thick. There was audio for the movie and a suitable laptop for our SKYPE call. I had come a long way from my first event at the QCBA. I was ready, or so I thought.

For the duration of that night I took a backseat role handing out fliers at the door until it was time for my five-minute speech, "You have all seen tonight Lakshimi's journey and story...." I began, sounding incredibly scripted and robotic. Yes, I was implementing everything I had been taught in my Decker communication course, minus the repeated pacing back and forth. I was big in my actions, but despite the absence of written notes I sounded as though I was reading from a script. In my opinion it was so bad that half way through my speech I discarded the mental script and improvised my remaining thoughts.

It became incredibly clear that night that I should stick to my day job and never consider a career in acting. In fact, it made me think about movie critics. I really didn't get it because on screen the casts entire role was scripted but often seemed to me to be so seamless, natural and realistic even if it was their tenth take.

Despite my not so stellar performance, that night was a tremendous success, topped off with an invitation by an FBI agent to bring my event to the FBI headquarters in Washington D.C. I was really on a high that evening because despite all the odds and adversities I had faced I had managed to singlehandedly pull off the event.

Night number two was at Google's Washington D.C. location with a slightly smaller crowd but a nice number in attendance, nonetheless. I was rather disappointed by the amount of no shows which included my landlord and her boyfriend, who I had communicated with that same afternoon.

That day I had no script instead I chose to improvise the entire time which was considerably better. Compared to the previous night there were no hiccups, so everything ran smoothly.

Night number three began with a bus journey from Washington D.C. to New York and then a long train ride to the Bronx. Despite the distance, I made good time, which relieved any pressure I may have felt.

Unlike the previous two nights this would be a considerably smaller affair despite the number of tickets that had been distributed. In my mind it was merely an illusion and would not reflect the actual number of attendees. That really was the least of my concerns however, because there was the bigger issue of two of my panelists cancelling at the last minute and one of my presenters arriving exceptionally late. This was a learning experience however, and the biggest thing I took away from that night was to always start events on time.

Things didn't get off to such a good start since my two remaining panelists were both male, neither of whom were transgender, abuse nor trafficking victims. Bearing in mind that most trafficked and exploited victims were female I knew that I had to even out the balance. Fortunately, a friend offered to jump in as a panelist, but one female simply wasn't enough. Begrudgingly I had to take on the role of female panelist number two. Even though I was really displeased about this decision I had no choice because it was a necessity.

That night the Holy Spirit took over. Someone asked a question and I shared so passionately from my heart to the extent that it seemed as though I was about to cry. I was filled with so much genuine emotion which was not something I'd made up for effect. The audience was really moved by my contributions and at the end of the night I was invited to speak at another event.

Despite my initial reluctance to be a panelist that night, I had no doubt in my mind that it was God's way of giving me a dress rehearsal ahead of my panel discussion in Tobago.

Surviving on very little sleep I awoke in the early hours of Saturday morning to make my way to JFK airport in New York. As daylight arrived I landed in Trinidad where I was met by a man I believed to be my brother in Christ and a new friend. How wrong I would be, as would be discovered a few weeks later, but for now I was blessed by this newfound acquaintanceship. Before leaving he provided me with mosquito cream, a small amount of local currency and the details of some budget hotels. I then boarded my 15-minute flight to Tobago and was soon headed to the Magdalena hotel.

The view from the lobby windows was absolutely beautiful, and as I stood there making a SKYPE call back home, I simply could not believe how truly blessed I was. I had waitressed for years in five-star hotels, but never in my wildest dreams did I envision being flown all expenses paid to a conference and staying at a luxury hotel in the Caribbean. This experience was like the kind of thing you read about in story books but that never actually happened in the real world.

Of course, I was here for a purpose, which meant all work and no play, especially since I was unprepared because despite being given months of notice, I had simply made myself busy doing nothing.

When the big day finally arrived, I was incredibly nervous and completely out of my depth. In my opinion it all went horribly wrong and I failed miserably at my delivery. I'd been allocated twenty minutes to present, with twelve of those minutes being taken up by two human trafficking videos. In the middle of the first video it was discreetly indicated to me that we would have to stop the video. Being as stubborn as ever I said that the video was almost finished so we should simply play it to the end; I was soon to discover that I was not going to have my way this time.

In fact, I was left feeling publicly humiliated when one of the judges angrily came over to me at the front of the room and demanded that we immediately cut the video. This completely threw me off kilter and I wanted the floor to swallow me up. In my mind things went from bad to worse with my poor performance and faltering responses.

Despite how confidently and coherently I had discussed human trafficking in the past from all the knowledge I'd garnered from attending countless lectures; seminars and conferences, I was completely out of my depth. I did the best that I could with the remaining time, before the other two panelists presented completely stealing the show.

The judges were all incredibly positive at the end and had not one bad word to say towards me. In my mind they were all lying, but then as judges what motivation would they have to lie?

Looking back at my first poor performance to now, I have really come a long way, so much so that I am a completely different person. From being intimidated by a room of thirty judges, to talking live on the T.V. and radio and to audiences exceeding eight hundred, the transformation has been truly astounding.

I do not consider myself an expert on the issue of human trafficking, but I have knowledge and experience that is far greater than the confines of most books. This would intimidate a number of people including some so-called experts who saw me as competition so much so that they had been unwilling to set aside personal differences and facilitate meaningful collaboration.

Then there were those who would feign excitement about the work that I do and exhibit pseudo-enthusiasm for collaboration or an upcoming speaking engagement. Each of those initial conversations had proved to be fruitless and devoid of substance, whilst the speaking engagements often came with challenges of their own.

Last minute cancellations were my greatest frustration because they failed to consider the value of my time which could have been invested elsewhere. The ease with which some people cancelled without excuse or explanation was in my mind the result of their lack of financial commitment. I am convinced that if my speaking engagements were chargeable the church auditoriums would have been packed, every room would have been filled, and cancellations would have been virtually nonexistent.

Understandably, things do happen outside of one's control but there seemed to be a consistent pattern of cancellations by Pentecostal churches. This was so much so that I had been advised unequivocally to decline any of their future requests for speaking engagements.

Looking back, cancellations really weren't that bad. Yes, I detested them like the plague, but the alternative was so much worse, which I knew only too well following an experience in Tobago.

What was most disappointing, about what had happened, was that the communication had gone through all the official channels, namely via e-mail. There was a paper trail which one would consider to be the hallmark of professionalism however; this was a far cry from the truth.

The Monday of that same week I had contacted one of the organizers concerning the plans for the following morning. I'd received no response. In the morning I sent multiple messages which were ignored, until I finally got a response advising me to consult my cab driver. I was confused. Considering that my arrangements for speaking did not concern my cab driver I was unclear as to what information he would be providing. He told me that the program was cancelled and that he was going home. When I then contacted the organizer and asked him why I had not been informed he responded, "I'm informing you now." I was floored, I could not believe I was experiencing such complete and utter disrespect and disregard for my time and person.

Three days later I arrived at the Youth Center to give my presentation. I felt very enthusiastic particularly as I'd been informed that the audience would greatly exceed the eight attendees from the previous day's session, plus my driver's reassurance that he too would be in attendance. The venue was just a stone's throw away from my home which ensured my prompt arrival at 2 p.m. Even so, this time I was prepared with my book in hand, after recently enduring a 1.5-hour car drive with only my cell phones to keep me occupied.

The room was empty which was customary for events in either of the two islands, therefore by 2.30 p.m. I was not the least bit concerned. At 3 p.m. with only one participant in attendance I was ready to leave. I messaged my driver since he had not stuck around as he'd indicated the day before only to be told that he was cooking and was twenty minutes away. By 3.30 p.m. impatience started to set in and I messaged my driver again only for my message to remain unanswered. I then began calling him but to no avail.

This entire time the only staff member present had failed to acknowledge me, let alone my excessive wait time, instead she remained deeply engrossed in a cell phone conversation.

By 4 p.m. I was quietly fuming so I told the member of staff that I needed to go home. She explained that the program should have been organized earlier in the day when there had been plenty of young people. Her suggestion was that I reschedule for another day to which I firmly refused. She then informed me that since she too had been unable to get hold of my driver, someone else would collect me, but that "They were really putting themselves out" because they were busy.

To say I felt insulted was an understatement. After having just wasted 2.5-hours of my time, the last thing I wanted to hear was that someone was putting themselves out by returning me home.

Long story short my original driver finally returned at 4.15 p.m. and less than ten minutes later I was back home, minus any kind of apology. I did what I deemed best in the situation and immediately blocked all of the organizers on WhatsApp and e-mail since this was not the time for grace. I had experienced blatant disrespect and disregard of my time, whilst being sat in an unsafe neighborhood for over two hours. Forgiveness was mandatory, but I vowed to never work with any of those individuals ever again. That 'professional' relationship was simply over before it had even started.

Such an experience was private, in the sense where, unless I shared with anyone what had transpired, it was as though it had never happened. This did not in any way alleviate how I felt, but my prayer was that it would be the first and last time I would ever endure anything of this nature.

Looking back, it really wasn't the worst that could have happened to me; it was really 'child's play' when I consider two incidents which were perpetuated by some former 'friends,' both allegedly Christian who took it upon themselves to try and sabotage my ministry. Suffice to say if God had not stepped in to defend me this book would have told a very different story because due to the severity of their malicious actions and character assassination my credibility and career as a respected attorney could have been completely destroyed.

Having my character attacked was nothing new because there were indeed individuals who had made it their mission to destroy my authenticity by vicious slander, gossip and public berating. One such incident occurred following yet another cancellation, but this time it was three hours before the allotted time. I was livid and rightly so, plus to make matters worse the establishment did not even have the decency to give me an explanation.

In the spirit of freedom of speech, I posted on my Facebook wall '#NoMoreCancellations and #NoMoreFreeSpeaking Engagements,' the latter of which, however, was merely an empty threat, since I did not have work authorization permitting me to get paid.

Jealously is a terrible thing, but sabotage is even worse. As many of my defenders commented on Facebook, I was sacrificing my time to give free advice to people who were not even my countrymen and instead of getting cheered on, people were trying to hinder the very message that I brought.

One such hindrance came from the Counter Trafficking Unit (CTU) who declined my request for funding and collaboration because "Limited human and financial resources do not permit us to assist in your efforts." Their e-mail dated January 16th, 2018, made it clear that I was on my own, so from that day forward the CTU became a dirty word in my life. I would avoid them like the plague but of course their name would always crop up since our line of work was so identical. I simply could not get away from them. The question I would always ask myself was, "Why aren't people asking the CTU why they haven't reached out to me instead of the other way around? After all, wouldn't they want to join forces with a freelance attorney doing similar work to them?" I did not have an answer to that question; but as it had stood more than a year ago that was exactly the situation, collaboration between myself and the CTU.

After leaving the judges' conference I had a week's stay planned in Trinidad, albeit without accommodation. The individual who had met me when I first arrived at the airport had worked out a quid pro quo arrangement. He had secured a place for me to stay but in return for the hospitality I was required to speak on human trafficking throughout the island. That seemed like a good deal because although my panel participation hadn't been very good, the pressure was now off, and I believed I was much more competent for the job ahead of me.

The head of CTU, Alana Wheeler, and I took our separate human trafficking presentations around to various schools on the island. We spoke from different perspectives, so our messages should have complemented each other. However, complement is probably not the most appropriate word where my presentation was concerned because I bored the kids to sleep. I was completely out of my comfort zone, I had never presented on human trafficking to children before, let alone children outside of the 'West.' It was of course a learning experience, one I was hoping I would not have to repeat.

Things were however about to change. As ridiculous as this sounds I did not know if I was allowed to use the word 'sex,' even though we were talking about sex trafficking. That was until I walked through the doors of 'Hugh Wooding Law School' and stood in front of a room full of adults. Looking back, it was definitely my 'breaking in' moment as once again my Decker Communication training paid off, and in such a big way that I would have done my instructors proud. I shared stories, described my exposures from travelling the world, and I comfortably used the word sex.

The following week when I should have been back in the States, I was still in Trinidad. In faith, I had spent my entire birthday money to change the date of my flight ticket and prolong my stay. Unfortunately, I was on my own because the CTU had relinquished their service but since I'd had my week of introductions I was ready for my launching pad. My intention was to continue sharing on human trafficking in conjunction with multiple screenings of 'SOLD.'

Things did not look promising at the start of my second week because my schedule was completely empty. This was about to change although I did not know it at the time, nor had I any idea that I would find myself flying back to Trinidad from New York less than a week later.

The following two weeks were like a whirlwind. Not only did I speak at various schools and churches but

I also had the opportunity to record my presentation so it could be made available for viewers online. In my mind, since I could not be everywhere at once, my video would serve the purpose of being shown in schools whilst I was overseas to ensure that my work continued. Unfortunately, my video did not have those desired results and over a year later had been viewed less than five hundred times.

That time spent however, proved not wasted because the recording also served as God's way of preparing me to speak in front of a camera, as less than 24-hours later I had my first live T.V. interview. As had become customary I was unprepared for the questions but still did exceedingly well.

Before I knew it, the two weeks had flown by and I was heading back to Asia to pursue a job prospect in South India.

On route I decided to spend some time in the Philippines in advance of my job start date. However, what was intended to be a few weeks became five months when the Indian job opportunity fell through. As this had not been part of the original plan I had to go on a visa run every thirty days. Since I was such a jet-setter, I used this as an opportunity to add to the list of countries I had visited.

On route to the Philippines I travelled from Trinidad to the U.S., then England, followed by a lengthy layover and tour in Qatar. I then visited Vietnam, Taiwan, Malaysia, Cambodia, and Singapore. This was all accomplished with a bank balance of zero and without the help of Visa or MasterCard, it was courtesy of Holy Spirit Air Miles.

Prior to the conclusion of my stay in the Philippines I gave a presentation on human trafficking, disclosures of abuse and the apprehension a criminal. This was another one of those 'out of my depth' moments and as had predominantly been the case I was unprepared. God came through for me as usual and the presentation was fantastic! Once again the Decker Communication course paid off and the police, social workers, barangay officials and Cebu's mayor left the room greatly educated and empowered. I had really come a long way from my first presentation at the judges' conference in Tobago and there was still plenty more room for growth.

Eight months later I was back for the fourth time to Trinidad and Tobago. Unlike my previous trips, nothing had been scheduled despite giving ample notice of my return and being promised speaking engagements by a number of individuals. Despite this initial setback, various opportunities arose and my time was indeed used productively.

One particular Sunday, that was a pivotal moment in my journey, was my morning presentation at 'Divine Encounter Fellowship Ministries International.' This was my first experience preaching to a packed church congregation which was a tremendous honor.

When I returned home that day and was going through my WhatsApp messages I was surprised to have received a 'text' from my former attorney. It had been four months since we'd last communicated and unfortunately due to circumstances outside of my control I was unable to solicit her services.

Nonetheless, we both picked up where we had left off, with me explaining that the registration of my Nonprofit was simply off the table at that point in time. She suggested I could instead register a limited liability entity, but that it would still require one other person for registration.

In my mind's eye this was not what God had wanted. I did not have that one person in my life, and I was unwilling to have any individual take on the role just for the sake of doing so. I explained this to my lawyer who suggested, "What about a sole trade that you could do by yourself?" I said, "That's perfect." Why? Just five days earlier I had received a prophetic word from someone, and the sole trade entity would have enabled that word to take fruition. Irrespective of that fact however, it looked like something that God would be agreeable with.

As we conversed the lawyer shared that it could be in my first and last name, provided that my name was available. It sounded like a good idea, especially as I was doing my speaking engagements and writing my book which would both come under the umbrella of my sole trade. She also told me that I could then apply for my work permit under the perimeter of the sole trade. It all made complete sense to me, thus enabling me to finally earn an income from my speaking engagements.

I asked the lawyer how long the entire process would take, and she said, "It should take six to eight weeks, but since you're famous in Trinidad it should all be very easy for you because you'll be requesting a work permit for you to do this work for a fee instead of volunteering your services unpaid as you've been previously doing." She then proceeded to explain the cost of the documentation which was incredibly cheap to file. She also shared that she would pay the fees for filing the sole trade and would also rescind charging for her service. She also said that if she had enough excess money remaining she would pay the work permit fees, whilst again waiving her attorney's fees.

I was astonished! I had not at all been expecting that. It felt like all my Christmases were coming at once! This was a moment where I felt the truth of the scripture that God will grant your heart's desire.[30]

Just as my friend had been saying the night before, "Trust God's timing," it was truly impeccable. To say I was ecstatic was an understatement, I was thoroughly overjoyed. I really felt like things were finally coming together, and in my mind I believed that against all the odds Trinidad would indeed become my new home at least for eight months of the year, with the Philippines for the remaining four.

What flashed across my mind at that time was the question that people always asked despite the fact that I'd already answered it, "Why did you decide to come to Trinidad?" To which my answer had always

---

[30] *"Delight thyself in the Lord; and He shall give thee the desires of thine heart."*
Psalm 37:4 (KJV)

remained the same, "God physically brought me here." This was not some sort of cliché response given to make myself seem 'overly' Christian; on the contrary it was simply the truth. Considering the challenges I frequently experienced in the country, it was truly a wonder that I kept coming back, in fact it was really nothing short of a miracle.

What saddened me most was the selfishness of people who called themselves Christian and instead of following the instructions in the Bible that says, when your brother is hungry give him bread,[31] they would take it upon themselves to give unsolicited 'advice.' To be honest I don't know if advice is even the right word, maybe a more appropriate term would be 'misdirection.'

The amount of so called Christians who told me to be careful and that my lifestyle was dangerous was too many to count. The interesting thing was that they were ever so concerned about my safety but consistently failed to provide me alternative transport or accommodation. The whole thing was really preposterous, almost laughable in fact. Their concern didn't go skin deep, instead they would encourage me to change my flight and wait standby; return to England; or come back at another time. All of which were misdirection and what I considered direct sabotage from the enemy.

---

[31] *"Suppose you have a friend, and you go to him at midnight and say, "Friend, lend me three loaves of bread.... And suppose the one inside answers, 'Don't bother me'. I tell you, even though he will not get up and give you the bread ... he will surely get up and give you as much as you need." Luke 11:5-8 (NIV)*

My most challenging trip to Tobago took place during the month of August a week before my birthday. I had been hosted there the previous month by a wonderful friend of a friend who told me I was welcome any time. Unfortunately, the 'any time' happened to be when her husband had suddenly been inflicted with a stroke. Without even being told, I knew that I'd no longer have a place to stay, at least for that period. With this knowledge in mind I reached out to everyone I knew to ask if they knew of someone who could host me.

The answer always came back "No" until the day finally drew around for my trip to Tobago. Things didn't start off too well with yet another cancellation. This one came as no surprise since the organizers had been resistant to the idea of providing me with a meal and transport. Now, considering that I was providing my services for free it was really the least they could do, but they clearly did not see it that way.

Unlike the previous cancellations, I did not react to the news despite how seriously inconvenienced I was. Not only was I taking a late-night flight to Tobago, but a program that had been organized with me in mind had to go ahead in my absence because of the timing of that earlier cancelled presentation.

That night was incredibly long, frustrating and riddled with confusion with things not getting any better the following morning. After a frantic couple of hours trying but failing to sleep, I was eventually able to doze off in the wee hours of the morning and without fail woke up without a voice and exhaustion rearing its head. Despite my situation that simply went from bad to worse with yet another cancellation, if I could even call it that, I still had to give God thanks for His provision.

Having a conversation with a local that day convinced me that my message was desperately needed in Tobago; because although C News had misrepresented me as saying, "Tobagonians too ambivalent on human trafficking,"[32] that really wasn't a far cry from the truth. In fact, it could simply have been the journalist's way of penning their own feelings whist using me as their scapegoat.

A lot of work still had to be done to educate the nation on human trafficking and although misquoted in that article I was standing by my opinion that many (but not all) of the people in Tobago were naïve on this particular issue. However, that naivety was something I was hoping to change, thus despite my frequent disappointment with the nation's people I was not willing to call it quits.

---

[32] C News, "Tobagonians Too Ambivalent On Human Trafficking, Prostitution", C TV, July 9, 2018, https://ctvtt.com/ctv/index-php/c-news/item/56916- tobagonians-too-ambivalent-on-human-trafficking-prostitution.

Trinidad and Tobago

◆

Four international trips to Trinidad and Tobago over a two year period saw my knowledge continue to grow as did my opportunities. Doors were opening in my life and not just for speaking engagements but also my frequent return to the country. On my third trip to Trinidad I was privileged to enjoy both stability and luxury in a huge bungalow courtesy of the Nonprofit organization '2 Cents Movement.'

One evening an employee of the organization happened to be in the garden whilst I was outside. We started talking and were soon joined by a young lady who during the course of the conversation revealed that she worked for Caribbean Airlines. Being brazen as ever I asked her if she could get me free flight tickets to which she responded she could not. The guy however, said that he had an airline voucher which he promptly retrieved from his room and gave to me.

The next day I went online with the resolve to use the voucher for flights between Trinidad and Tobago, but the valued dollar amount was excessive. I then considered flights from England to Trinidad but to my disappointment the airline no longer flew that route. I then settled on flights between New York and Trinidad.

Now I was supposed to move to India on July 1st for a job opportunity but despite my love for the country, I didn't want to move to that specific location. I had the flight voucher with a July expiration date which led me to consider the possibility that God would return me to Trinidad in the summer.

The sales agent from Caribbean Airlines called me promptly at 11 a.m. and we began looking at flight dates. Unfortunately, the flight on July 1st far exceeded the cost of the voucher so we checked earlier dates in late June until we settled on June 21st.

Now my mistaken belief had been that I would be getting a free flight, however, no such luck as I was informed I was required to pay the applicable taxes. I was confused; if God was returning me to Trinidad and not sending me on the July 1st to India then I needed a clear confirmation that He was indeed directing me to forfeit my paid job. I therefore needed some time to think and pray.

My money was very thin on the ground but I happened to have an envelope with the words 'flight ticket' written on the outside. I believed there was 300TT dollars inside, but I needed 500TT dollars to pay Caribbean Airlines.

I said to God through Jesus Christ directly, "Maybe if there's 500TT dollars in the envelope it's a sign from you, but if there is not 500TT dollars then it's not a sign." I opened the envelope and removed 50TT dollars, 100TT dollars, 150TT dollars, and then a total of 500TT dollars. "It's a sign from God," I exclaimed!

I gave the money to the lady from Caribbean Airlines and the following day she contacted me to confirm that my flight was booked.

Exactly four months later I flew from New York to Trinidad for only $20.00 U.S! That's the God that I serve who reduced the airfare tax from 500TT dollars to 140TT dollars and flew me from one continent to another for less than the price of a vegan sandwich.

Each time I returned my experiences differed from the previous trip, and I sincerely believed that God was giving me continual upgrades. My first year was my 'breaking in' moment, just getting a feel of the country and culture. In all transparency the children actually fell asleep in my presentations and even I was bored. I was partnered with the Counter Trafficking Unit and spoke alongside Alana Wheeler who had outshone me.

I tried but sometimes failed at being culturally sensitive and politically correct, but unsurprisingly I couldn't please everyone which was never my intention. The only person I intended to please was myself and as long as God was happy that was really all that mattered.

One individual, who had invited me to speak twice at their establishment, made what I considered to be a very ignorant remark that, "Using the word cookie is too graphic and not culturally sensitive." That was in reference to the story, "Daddy is eating my cookie." I had shared that very same story multiple times on the T.V. and radio, in schools and churches and not one person had ever expressed those sentiments to me whether verbally or in writing. On the contrary I was always well received; invited to speak again, and told how "Fantastic, enlightening and informative" my presentations were and that it had "Exceeded expectations."

I did not need or require validation from anyone but as I was particularly self-critical of everything I did, I was always blessed by the affirmation and gratitude of my audience. Since I did my speaking engagements for free I was not spurred on by money or gifts. Instead it was the words of hope, encouragement and positivity that really added value to my work.

I was actually honored to meet a couple aged ninety-two and eighty-four who had thanked me for my presentation, sharing how much they had thoroughly enjoyed it. I actually got a photo together with them to document the momentous experience. That couple had been alive for decades, having grown up and been part of an era where the word 'sex' was completely unspoken, notwithstanding many of the other controversial topics I would discuss. After being told previously by an individual that 'cookie' was too graphic, I was beyond blessed by this couples praise.

My presentations were always changing because I learned from my audience. There were of course many consistencies whenever I would present but the more exposure I got particularly to local stories of abuse, the greater the need became for adaption. Having spoken with a police officer about my 'cookie' story she disclosed to me the adverse effects of using the words "Cookie, butterfly, pumpkin etc." to identify the male or female genitals.

First of all, as I am sure we can all agree, most children would disclose to a peer or friend at school, just like that 7-year-old girl who I consistently referred to. She came to school and said, "Daddy is eating my cookie."

Please understand that I am 100% unbiased but having read newspaper articles and court case documents detailing the sexual acts a defendant wishes to perform or did indeed perform on a child, "Daddy is eating my cookie," is simply child's play.

I can further validate my opinion because having shared this story repeatedly, the audience's reaction was almost always laughter or even hysterics so much so that I had to warn children prior to sharing the story that, "This is not funny, I do not want to see anyone laughing." Despite my forewarning, every time I would mention the word 'cookie,' there would usually still be a number of smirks. Why? Because it wasn't anywhere close to being graphic. After all, if it had indeed been graphic, why didn't anyone at the time understand that the child was referring to being sexually abused? My theory is simply that the word 'cookie' is not the universal term for the female genitals.

The police have a job to investigate the crimes perpetrated against victims but we the public hinder that investigation in so many ways. One such hindrance was not using the universal terms for genitals with the children in our care or supervision.

I would always encourage my audience that if they were really uncomfortable talking about certain parts of the male or female anatomy that they should simply spell out the name of the body parts, or use commonly known terms like genitals, private parts, or sexual organs.

Being uncomfortable talking about sex would not stop child abuse from happening, instead in my mind it went some way towards explaining why there was often so much shame and embarrassment talking about the body, which resulted in such excessive delays in disclosures.

My desire for Trinidad and Tobago was to give a voice to the voiceless. This probably sounds really clichéd, but it is indeed one of the reasons for writing this book. It is also why I created male and female, "Can You Keep A Secret?" Facebook groups. I understand that the success of those groups could be very slow and gradual primarily because of fear.

Many men and women, boys and girls in the nation are not ready to publicly share their secrets but instead remain in an existence of shame, guilt, self-blame and bondage. Even the offer of an anonymous disclosure had yet to instill any courage in the survivors I had met to share their story. This saddens me because I have observed the reactions of people whenever I disclosed my story of sexual abuse and it had always been one of complete shock.

I am a firm believer that a person's past does not have to dictate their future, therefore whenever I stood in front of an audience in my business suit delivering a very eloquent message people were often surprised because they did not expect me to survive in the way that I did. When I detailed the ways an abuse survivor was often affected, particularly concerning promiscuity or prostitution it almost seemed as though this became the expectation. People were further taken aback when I shared my values of celibacy and desire to save sex until marriage.

For those who were gullible and easily misled by my strong boundaries and values concerning sex they would be under the false assumption that I have been single from birth. In fact, I had a Filipino friend who went around telling people at a singles retreat how 'innocent' I was and that I had been single all the days thus far of my earthly life. I will dispel this myth once again. I have not been single since birth but going to an all-girls secondary school that would have been easily attainable.

Unfortunately, as a result of being abused, despite knowing that I have been "Healed in Jesus name," I have struggled with insecurity and low self-esteem. I was bullied at school, called cat eyes and ugly which I continued to believe into my adult life (irrespective of any male attention I received).

My Christian faith has always dictated the way I lived my life, so I have never had a backslidden season during my journey with God. I have however displeased God with many of the decisions that I made but He has always been gracious to forgive me.

I have never had any motivation to keep a record of past relationships but the one commonality that existed was that the duration never exceeded three months. One of my recent relationships was a joke for more reasons than one; the most important of all is that it should never have started, albeit it exceeded my relationship from the previous year which lasted 24-hours.

Certain values had been instilled in me throughout my life, just as the word of God says, *"Train up a child in the way he should go: and when he is old, he will not depart from it."*[33] My mother set a strong foundation and even as an adult there were certain things I still would not do. I did not have a close relationship with her but when I tried to extend this olive branch of a complement it would fall flat with her response that she couldn't stop me if I made a bad decision or came home pregnant outside of marriage.

I have been very blessed in life by my various exposures and experiences. I read a lot, listen attentively, observe and then formulate my decisions accordingly. Christian dating books took over when my mum 'relinquished' her parenting of me. She was not a Christian when I was growing up but understood the importance of my regular attendance at church. Coming home pregnant was never an option, instead church taught me celibacy.

Life has been a learning experience filled with so many variables. My intention is to reflect Christ in everything that I say and do and the decisions that I make. Outside of 'dating' I have been focused on my relationship with Christ and not religion. Inside the realm of 'dating' I

---

[33] Proverbs 22:6 (KJV)

was incredibly legalistic. Understanding the simple fact that men and women were wired differently, I implemented strict boundaries in my 'dating' life.

The first boundary I have was that I do not date, especially after having been on dates with guys I had zero interest in. There have been two experiences that were complete torture which changed my willingness to date. Aside from that, the world's view of dating was vastly different from mine, hence my use of ''. I do not want to be in anyway misleading because there have been occasions when I had gone out with a male individual in what could be perceived as a date, however, society's connotations with this word has made me very uncomfortable using it.

At my young, intentionally undisclosed age, I have been waiting for marriage. In fact, I recently placed a post on Facebook, 'I do not want a free ride or boyfriend. #Please Stop Asking!!' When I created this post, I felt as though I was lying because sometimes I did need a free ride and in fact I did want a boyfriend, just not in the way the world perceived.

Well, truth be told I do want a husband but I have accepted that there is a process before the "I do," a process that includes courtship for marriage, not a boyfriend for fun. If I was ever blessed to have a boyfriend I do not think he would even consider our relationship fun since the only physical contact allowed would be side hugs and holding hands.

As I had told my boyfriend of six days "It's not Christmas day yet, it's only January." This was figuratively speaking of course with Christmas day referring to the wedding ceremony. On Christmas day we open our presents not before, if it's January you have to exercise the fruit of patience[34] and wait. On the contrary, if you open your Christmas presents ahead of Christmas day, there'd be nothing to open on Christmas day.

That is the way that I look at courtships and relationships. The Bible says, *"Marriage is honorable in all, ... and the bed undefiled,"*[35] therefore on 'Christmas day' you would enjoy this present in all its fullness. A lot of people do not look at it this way, including many Christians who would just wait until 'Easter' meaning the engagement and then prematurely open their 'Christmas' present.

Although unmarried I am convinced that the best sex would be in marriage and since God designed us, His instructions are our manual. Just as the designer of a car provides a manual, if we do not read or at least peruse it, we would try and drive the car from the passenger seat.

The sad reality is that there are numerous men and women, boys and girls who have been sexually violated. As the Bible says, *"Do not arouse or awaken love until it so desires."*[36] When this happens because of something done by you or done to you it changes you (often stealing your innocence). I have met victims and survivors of sexual abuse who were promiscuous,

---

[34] Galatians 5:22 (KJV)

[35] Hebrews 13:4 (KJV)

[36] Song of Solomon 8:4 (KJV)

prostituted, lesbian, gay, transgender or living a life of celibacy. People are obviously affected differently by the violations they have experienced but I firmly believe that despite what was stolen we are all survivors.

As a Christian there are certain lifestyles and behaviors that I would never advocate, but my intentions have always been to value and respect others irrespective of the choices that they made. Therefore, whenever I presented I would always make reference to sex after marriage and not before; this included not watching pornography before (or after) marriage; and a strong message of discouragement from making pornography.

I have always been a firm believer that we must guard our hearts and minds by the things we expose ourselves to, and the relationships that we form. It is for this reason that I do not own or watch T.V., instead I spend my free time reading fiction (but even with that I have to tread carefully since many books are laden with unnecessarily explicit sex scenes).

Whenever I would present the first things people observed were my appearance, clothing and hair, followed by my voice and accent. People would judge me instantly; creating a picture in their head about who I was, how much money I had in the bank, the way I lived my life and my relationship status. Unless they had seen or heard me speak before, they would always be 100% wrong.

I could only imagine some of the things that they thought about me and much of it would concern my supposed wealth (as an attorney) especially considering how frequently I travel. Then the rings on my wedding finger, would give the impression that I am married, plus the fact that people didn't always pay full attention to what I said so they would sometimes congratulate me on being married and having a 4-year-old.

There have been times more often than not that I wish I was married. Not so sure I am ready for the responsibility of a 4-year-old, but I deeply long for a Godly husband who would love and care about me. Not only was I sick of the unwanted male attention I consistently received, but my life has been incredibly lonely. Presenting in front of a room full of people, receiving an enthusiastic applause and then walking away to an empty row of chairs was incredibly depressing. Speaking on human trafficking and child sexual abuse should not consume my life; because just as Joyce Meyers and Joel Osteen have huge ministries, they also have a spouse and family.

What people failed to realize was that I did not choose this ministry, it chose me the day I was sexually abused.

Consequently, a life of singleness was something I greatly despise because it is not what I would have chosen for myself. Sacrificing my own happiness for the expense of others was not something I was willing to do, and I have no qualms in sharing my willingness to call it quits. Being everyone's super hero was demanding and draining, notwithstanding I've had problems of my own, but no one willing to listen. Despite over four hundred contacts in my phone, whenever I would have a problem, no one even cared. Instead people only took interest in my life when they could get something from me, namely a free presentation.

Ten or more flights a year have made me the envy of many, but my life was really not half as 'glamorous' as it might seem. I had no one to talk to or share experiences with, to watch my belongings as I went for a swim or enjoy dinner dates with.

Despite this, there have been countless individuals who wanted to have the luxury of all my travels but had no idea about my backpacker lifestyle. I have met so many people around the world who said that they wanted to be a missionary, so they could travel. I would always say the same thing, "Being a missionary starts in your home; at your workplace and among your friends. You don't need to go abroad to be a missionary."

In my opinion those people had impure motives and thus would never become international missionaries. God looks at our hearts;[37] therefore if you have a passion for travelling you should simply say that, instead of spiritualizing it and lying that you want to be a missionary.

I love travelling and God took my love of travelling and gave me a message to take around the world. I love serving others and volunteering for free. Likewise, God used that love and passion and made it global. It has taken a lot of character development to take me from the way I thought and acted to the person I became.

---

[37] 1 Samuel 16:7 (KJV)

All of my experiences have shaped me and the way I think, which is unique when compared to the average individual.

Something is missing however, and that is my future husband. His absence does not place me in a position of desperation because if it had I would have been married already, to the 'wrong guy.' Instead I don't think about it, but absolutely hate National Singles Day on February 14th, and have become increasingly uncomfortable around most couples especially when there was any PDA (public display of affection) or couples' discussion.

Time and time again I'd been deceived into believing that I would get married soon but the soon had yet to materialize many years later. It has eventually reached to the point where I am sick of prophesies concerning my single status because its failure to materialize has led me to deem it lies.

I have however, been pleading to God a lot recently particularly in the presence of one of my 'uncles.' Since the Bible says, *"And call no man your father upon the earth: for one is your Father, which is in heaven."*[38] Whenever I met Godly men with the nature of a 'father' instead of using the 'F' word, I would call them 'uncle.'

One such 'uncle' had heard me pleading repeatedly to God concerning my singleness and on one night in particular I'd said to him, "I just want to meet my

---

[38] Matthew 23:9 (KJV)

husband. Why can't we be friends? It's not like we are going to get married overnight, rather you become friends first. I know you are not God, but why can't I just meet him?"

The next day I believed I did! That was however, until four months later when for the second time that year I met a different guy and was certain that he was my future husband.

With guy number one I'd only shared my experience with five people in Trinidad and three friends in the Philippines. My Filipino friends were more excited about him than I was or maybe I'd disguised my excitement a lot better since it actually took me two hours to get to sleep after meeting him.

So, what convinced me at the time that he was the guy I was going to marry, since I'd been convinced countless times before? One word, everything (or so I thought)!

The more I got to know him, the stronger my conviction became however it was a secret that I had to keep between myself and God. It was simply not the right time, but I had complete confidence in this guy that when it was the right time he would know and communicate accordingly. As a person that always takes the lead and initiates I had to take a back-seat role which wasn't exactly easy for me but I knew that this would be one of those times where I would have to exhibit patience.

I had asked God to meet my future husband and be friends and so that was exactly what I thought I had got, friendship. In my mind's eye, if I had simply been more patient I would have met him at a time when we were both ready for courtship, instead there were a number of speed bumps to bypass along the way to that destination.

As time would later reveal, those speed bumps were instead an indicator that he was indeed not the right guy, and certainly not the marriage material that I had been looking for. In fact, truth be told, what I had first considered speed bumps could best be likened to red flags.

All throughout that time I was still single but considered myself to be taken, therefore whenever someone asked me if I was really looking for a hot, single Christian guy I told them that statement was merely a joke and I was unavailable.

Someone had told me earlier in the year that my future husband would not be from England, so when I met this guy his 'foreign' status validated what I'd been told. Notwithstanding his nationality, I felt as though God had been 'grooming' me to accept the idea of living in Trinidad and Tobago, in fact in that very same week someone had made a 'joke' saying as much and I had simply raised my eyebrows in quiet ascent.

Things people had spoken to me about the kind of guy I needed to marry appeared to be evident in this individual. However, looks were incredibly deceiving because as time slowly revealed, he was not the person I had first believed him to be.

He was very impatient, insensitive, overly direct and sometimes rude, and therefore really lacked in the 'fruit'[39] department which is where prospective future husband number two came in.

We met when I least expected it, in one of the last places I would have ever been looking for a potential spouse. Our story appeared to be amazing and I was hoping we would have had a much better ending than that of 'Prospective Husband #1' a.k.a counterfeit spouse.

The nature of the work that I have been doing was highly sensitive with many hidden dangers; consequently, I was discouraged or rather forbidden from speaking on human trafficking for a season of time. Despite this instruction, I promptly disregarded it for the mere fact that my obedience was always first and foremost to God rather than man (or woman). Sadly, the doors of opportunity that opened for speaking opportunities were few and far between, but I was grateful for them, nonetheless. It was in fact through my obedience to God that I met future husband number two, who I shall refer to as GA (The Genuine Article).

As a result of my 'disobedience' to refrain from speaking on human trafficking I met a female survivor of sexual abuse. She sought counsel from me, and I did my best to provide her with a support system and shoulder to cry on. Through this individual I met GA.

Now, as a result of my 'missionary' type lifestyle I

---

[39] *Supra* 18

frequently solicited services from complete strangers for free. This was one such occasion when I had been looking for someone to assist me. The help originally came from a guy in Trinidad until he came up against some time-consuming obstacles.

The female survivor that I mentioned previously gave me the contact number of GA (without first getting his consent to do so). I had messaged him, "Hi," but once the Trinidadian came on board I didn't pursue any further communication with GA, despite his frequent messages.

When the Trinidadian relinquished his service, I picked up where I had started with GA who agreed to assist me. I later found out that his initial understanding was that he was undertaking a simple job in hand, only for him to later expend three long days completing the task.

GA later shared with me three stories of how he had heard the voice of God, and his obedience on each occasion resulted in a bigger blessing than he could have ever anticipated. Interestingly story number three concerned me and went something like this:

GA had a mutual understanding with the female survivor that she needed his permission before giving out his number. On this occasion she didn't do so but gave me his number without consent. Now, since GA was very business minded, whenever he provided a service to a client he would always discuss and agree the price up front. With me however, he didn't do so because God had instructed him not to. Whilst he was doing the work, what had begun as a simple task became more complicated and thus time consuming. GA began to lose interest in the work and did not want to do his best, but God rebuffed him, instructing him to give his best.

Unbeknownst to me GA had been deep in conversation with God the whole time he'd been assisting me. Nothing really surprised me, so when he did the work without asking for any money upfront I just expected that God would pay him in full.

Three days later when GA had completed everything he asked me how I would compensate him, to which I responded that I would bake a cake for him and take him for dinner. I proceeded to give my sob story of being an unpaid volunteer and thus that was the best way for me to show my gratitude.

A few days later we finally met, but that was after I had changed the venue which resulted in GA enduring an almost two hour commute and a six hour wait. This was our first time meeting, and we hit it off instantly. At one point I'd misheard that he was a year older than me, and almost choked on my food. I couldn't think straight for a moment as I pondered between GA and the former 'future husband.'

Whilst we were talking I brought up 'future husband' number one with GA mentioning his current prospective. After listening I very boldly told him that she was not for him, that he should not settle and instead should remain single for the right person (which I didn't realize at the time was me). I then explained that I had a 'ministry' where people in 'wrong' relationships both male and female usually broke up with their girlfriend or boyfriend within 24-hours of meeting me.

When we parted company that day I hugged GA twice. I'm not too sure why I did that at the time since we were both 'unavailable,' plus the fact that GA was much younger than me.

We continued to communicate daily via WhatsApp with GA having me in stitches. I have no idea why, but I kept making very overt flirtatious comments. So overt that I was convinced GA was going to run away (despite the fact that he never did). It did get 'worse' however, when I suggested that me and GA become companions and enter into a 'contractual' relationship.

This was the first time I'd ever come up with such an idea, but I thought it made sense and I liked it. I suggested to GA that since we were both 'unavailable' we should become companions, therefore if anyone asked us if we were in a relationship we could honestly say "Yes." The idea was for us to be companions until we began a relationship with our 'significant other.' GA was in agreement of the idea and said he'd make it official when we next met.

A week later I proceeded to make my way to the meeting point that GA had suggested. On the way there, the wheel on the first bus exploded; then the driver stole my money by refusing to refund me. When I got on the second bus it broke down, then on the third bus I was stuck in traffic. I did not know what was going on and began to worry that either God was stopping me from going or it was hindrances from the devil.

When I finally arrived in one piece, albeit shaken up, GA decided to make our relationship official but instead of becoming 'companions' we actually began courting as boyfriend and girlfriend.

Unfortunately, our romantic relationship was really, really, really short lived and I was heartbroken, twice. I had fallen deeply in love with GA and I knew that I wanted to spend the rest of my life with him. As far as I was concerned he was not a counterfeit but was everything I had spent years praying for.

My friends and acquaintances, however, were of two minds with the majority leaning towards the negative. I refused to adhere to their advice and opinions which were based purely on the short duration of our relationship.

As I shared with one of my few supporters, God was not a joking God. I did not believe that after over a decade of praying, God would bring the most 'amazing' guy into my life just for my heart to get trodden all over. That made no sense to me, and like someone told me,

"Even Joseph wanted to break up with Mary.[40] When in the Bible did any Christian have things easy?" How true a statement that really was but was little comfort because I was surrounded by Job's friends.[41]

After the breakup I went through a myriad of emotions, I blocked GA (for a day); I cried; quit Christianity; and contemplated suicide. The good news was that I became Christian again after a mere eight hours and righted my relationship with God. In case it isn't completely obvious, I made GA an idol, which was probably why God removed him because as a friend reminded me, God is a jealous God.[42]

Valentine's Day was fast approaching, and it would be yet another year as a single. In faith I had already purchased and written in GA's Valentine's card and had been putting together some plans for its delivery.

Despite my belief concerning 'future husband' number one, my beliefs often failed me, but this time I truly believed that things were different. Unlike the guys before, GA was the first relationship I had ever had

---

[40] *"This is how the birth of Jesus the Messiah came about: His mother Mary was pledged to be married to Joseph, but before they came together, she was found to be pregnant through the Holy Spirit. Because Joseph her husband was faithful to the law, and yet did not want to expose her to public disgrace, he had in mind to divorce her quietly. But after he had considered this, an angel of the Lord appeared to him in a dream and said, "Joseph son of David, do not be afraid to take Mary home as your wife, because what is conceived in her is from the Holy Spirit."* Matthew 1:18-20 (NIV)

[41] Job 1- 36 (NIV)

[42] *"Do not worship any other god, for the LORD, whose name is Jealous, is a jealous God."* Exodus 34:14

where I was not unequally yoked.[43] This was huge for me; even more so because of the age gap, and since men were considered the head of the house[44] it was required for the husband to be knowledgeable of the Bible so that he could lead his wife.

GA ranked top points where this was concerned, he was so wise that I would often call him my teacher or guru, and comment that I was often confused as to which one of us was older. This also made GA predictable, because I could always find the answer to any question I had for him in the Bible.

I was convinced that GA heard directly from God and thus he wouldn't move without His consent. His wisdom was often overwhelming, and I was usually blown away by his knowledge. Our conversations were never competitions, but I would always say, "You win," since I could never argue with God's word. Surprisingly, despite our vast cultural differences we shared the same Christian beliefs; had both read the entire Bible and had identical understandings of the things of God.

GA was the most spiritually beautiful guy I had ever had the privilege of meeting, because his beauty was much more than skin deep. Not only did we have identical goals and visions, but we thought the same,

---

[43] *Supra* 7

[44] *"For the husband is the head of the wife as Christ is the head of the church, his body."* Ephesians 5:23

were incredibly alike and in sync with one another. For the first time in my life I believed in soul mates because I had actually met mine.

GA was absolutely EVERYTHING I had been praying to God for in a spouse and so much more. He was still an imperfect human being, a Christian that was under construction, but I knew I had met the love of my life.

Unlike all my prior crushes or relationships this was the first time that I had ever felt secure in a relationship. I trusted GA implicitly and had no insecurities as to why he was with me. I believed that he was the guy I was going to marry, and at the time he believed that too.

Despite how premature our courtship was we discussed absolutely everything and were 100% on the same page concerning our future. Unlike the average couple, it wasn't usually until a year or more that they had 'the talk,' and only then after emotions and time has been invested did they realize that they had nothing in common. GA and I were therefore different because we laid all our cards out on the table and thus discovered that we wanted exactly the same things.

For two people from opposite ends of the world, with the tiny matter of an age gap to share the same love for God, identical visions, goals and desires there had to be more to that than meets the eye. What some would consider coincidence, for me was God-appointment.

I obviously did not know the end of the story, so all I could do was pray for the restoration of my relationship with GA stronger than it was before. I was not delusional and knew that there were better guys than GA, but did I want better? I wanted God's best and firmly believed GA was exactly that.

By GA's own admission his prayer life improved since meeting me; the 'prospective' and all other female distractions disappeared out of his life; not to mention the immense favor he always had whenever we'd meet. Together we demonstrated the scripture, "iron sharpens iron,"[45] and for that I am thankful. Although far too brief we'd had a really beautiful relationship that I struggled to accept was over. It seemed however, I may have been gravely deceived because just days before National Singles Day on February 14th the potential of someday rekindling a romantic relationship together appeared to be well and truly severed.

The guy I once considered to be GA, the 'Genuine Article' would be better described as 'Grossly Artificial.' He appeared to be a liar, a deceiver, and a wolf in sheep's clothing which I only discovered after a week's 'fast' of communication. This fast was something I had been considering for some time, especially when we hadn't spoken for two days and had both missed each other. Although the saying goes, 'absence makes the heart grow fonder,' the real reality was that it may instead make or break a relationship as it did here.

Eight days after I began my communication 'fast' I

---

[45] *"As iron sharpens iron, so one person sharpens another."* Proverbs 27:17

89

finally contacted 'Grossly Artificial,' who had actually sent me a PDF book on marriage the night before. When I asked him when and where he had received it, he told me the previous day but kept mum about the deliverer.

When I pried a little further he kept saying, "In due time," which was incredibly misleading under the circumstances. In fact, because of his evasiveness I was of the impression that an older lady at church had given him the book for us to both study together. Instead, he eventually but somewhat reluctantly revealed that it was from a colleague at work. Through further inquiry he also shared that he had "slowly growing and definite" feelings for this girl who he'd only known for eight days, having met her shortly after our break up.

I was completely floored that the guy I believed was the love of my life, had found a rebound that quickly, despite telling me that he was not ready for a relationship and I should wait for him. To say I was shocked was a complete understatement, this was heartbreak number two from the same guy who further decided to rub salt in the wounds by repeatedly telling me "don't wait for me Juanita," as though I was a robot that could turn my feelings on and off by the press of a switch.

Once again, it was history repeating itself with me pursuing a relationship that left me completely devastated. The little solace I took was from the story of Joseph who had wanted to break up with his fiancée Mary when he found out that she was pregnant (with

Jesus).[46] That was not how the story ended however, because God intervened by sending an angel to hinder Joseph's 'plan.'[47] Unfortunately for me I had not been so lucky, and although I had witnessed countless success stories of my friends, the truth was that I doubted whether I too would ever follow suit and get my heart's desire of marriage.[48]

This book, however, was another one of my lifelong desires which prior to writing I had discussed with a fellow new author who actually inspired me to put pen to paper and exceed her 65-page autobiography. I asked her how my book should end since I did not have a paid job, nor was I married or even completely established. She simply encouraged me to write and so I did. She was my inspiration, I had been writing stories from the age of ten however many were incomplete especially when writers block set in at the age of twenty.

This book is 100% God inspired! My friend wrote a 65- page book in three months. I intended to exceed her page limit in less than a month without consistent daily writing. In less than a fortnight I had accomplished forty-nine pages and still had seventeen days to go

---

[46] *Supra* 40

[47] *But after he had considered this, an angel of the Lord appeared to him in a dream and said, "Joseph son of David, do not be afraid to take Mary home as your wife, because what is conceived in her is from the Holy Spirit. She will give birth to a son, and you are to give him the name Jesus, because he will save his people from their sins." All this took place to fulfill what the Lord had said through the prophet: "The virgin will conceive and give birth to a son, and they will call him Immanuel" (which means "God with us"). When Joseph woke up, he did what the angel of the Lord had commanded him and took Mary home as his wife."* Matthew 1:20-24

[48] *Supra* 30

(excluding Sundays of course since that was my day of rest).

November 30th, 2018, had been my publication date so that my book would be available ahead of Christmas. I had been talking to lots of publishers and editors in the two islands and had sent out over four hundred e-mails to lawyers, judges and those in the anti-trafficking world concerning my book.

Someone had reached out to me on Facebook after hearing about the work I had been doing educating and empowering people on the issue of human trafficking. They were part of a church body and wanted to discuss collaboration. During the course of our conversation they mentioned in passing that they had a publishing company in the U.S; I believed it was a sign from God and was really excited.

They continued to explain that they had been in operation for four years and had helped authors construct their material into a workbook with questions for discussion at the conclusion of each chapter. They also explained that they even offered ghostwriters whereby I could record my books' contents, and someone else would type it. Once the book was spoken or written by me they would publish it and create a website for readers to receive further training and education on the content of the book. They would then help authors to become public speakers.

I was amazed! This seemed absolutely perfect since I was already a public speaker who wanted to educate people on human trafficking. I was ecstatic, that was until they discussed the price. For a ghost writer the cost was $5,000.00, and for submission of my written manuscript approximately $2,000.00. The cost was simply astronomical. I had been hoping they would have said free, but no such luck.

A local publisher in Trinidad however had been in communication with me around the same time and he had offered publication services for $1,500.00. It was cheaper than the U.S. publishers but still an amount I simply could not afford. That was until the publisher saw my 1-minute video introduction, and realized I "Was no ordinary individual," and offered me a $500.00 discount. This was a tremendous blessing, but I still didn't know where I would obtain the remaining $1,000.00.

Since I hold a firm belief in the power of prayer, I began praying that God would grant me the finances to pay $2,000.00 for the American publishers to publish my book.

Morning and night I would read from my prayer journal out loud but to no avail. I did not give up hope however but continued praying.

A number of weeks later I had a radio interview on Power 102FM. It was my first radio interview in a while, so I was looking forward to the opportunity to share with the public about human trafficking. Before I knew it the time had gone by and the program had come to an end.

When I got the chance to scroll through my phone I saw that a number of people had messaged me expressing how touched they had been by the program. One such person was the Trinidad publisher. He shared how he had been watching the live broadcast online and was amazed at my faith and testimony. He had been so touched by the message I had given that he told me he would be publishing this book for free.

I was shocked! When I read the message, I had to shout hallelujah out loud right there in the radio station. My prayers had paid off; from a $500.00 discount to free, I could not believe it. Unbelievable was really an understatement. When I had arrived at the radio station one and a half hours ahead of schedule, I had no idea that I would be leaving there with an answer to my prayer.

In the space of a week I had been blessed yet again with answered prayers … stability, free book publication…. I simply could not get enough of God's provisions.

My journey was far from over; in fact, it was only just beginning. As the year was slowly drawing to a close and 2019 began its fast approach I was convinced that my seventh year as a volunteer would be different. I had been pleading to God and fellow believers that I wanted stability; I was sick of living the way that I had for the past six years and wanted the finances that would bring about what I so desperately desired.

I would never stop travelling even after I eventually got married but I would be willing to travel less, instead of eight countries a year, maybe cut that in half to three or four. India is my second home and I would always stop there whenever I was on route to or from the Philippines. The Philippines is the place where I wanted to build my orphanage and adopt street children from. New York is the place that I am licensed as an attorney and England is the place that I would get the necessary visas from.

Trinidad and Tobago were never chosen by me, but they were chosen by God. It was the closest I could get to my parents' home land Jamaica, so that gave me contentment. I love the food and the Indian influence. The country has given me the best of both worlds, Asia and the West and I was willing to embrace it for all it had to offer.

Although my answer was still that I didn't like the country, I certainly didn't hate it, how could I? After all I would publish my book there and establish my career there. Those are two things I am truly thankful for. Eventually I am certain I would be sure to like it since it was a place that had brought me tremendous fulfillment and more. The things I had been searching for found me when I followed God's leading in January 2017 and against my better judgment participated as a panelist at the National Bar Association's Judge's Conference and for that opportunity I am truly thankful.

List of Trinidadian Speaking Engagements

♦

The following is not an exhaustive list of all the various platforms I've had to bring my education and empowerment message in the islands of Trinidad and Tobago:

Televised Interviews:

- ACTN The Voice
- CTV
- CNC3
- Tobago Inspirational Network
    - o Impact to Impart
- Islamic Broadcasting Network
- IETV
    - o Human Trafficking
    - o Rape and Violence
    - o Child Sexual Abuse
- Tobago Channel 5
    - o Rise and Shine
    - o Weekend Digest
- Trinity TV

- TTT
- TV6
- TV Jaagriti

Radio Interviews:

- Pulse 89.5FM
- Tambrin 92.7FM
- I-Dependency 95.5FM
- Isaac 98.1FM
- Power 102FM
- Resurface Broadcasting Network
- Sky 99.5FM
- SMASH Radio
- Talk City 91.1FM
- Vibe City 105.1FM
- Word 107.1FM

Newspaper Articles:

- Newsday
- The Guardian
- The Mirror

Educational Establishments: Schools:

- Arima North Secondary Comprehensive
- Bishops Anstey School
- Bishops Centenary College
- Bishops Secondary School
- Carapichaima East Secondary School
- Cascade School For The Deaf

List of Trinidadian Speaking Engagements

- Chaguanas North Secondary School
- Chaguanas South Secondary school
- Corpus Christi School
- Diego Martin Central Secondary School
- Gasparilllo Secondary School
- Harmon High School
- Holy Faith Covenant Penal School
- Holy Name Covenant School
- La Horquetta Government Primary School
- Lakshimi Girl's Hindu College
- Matura Secondary School
- Moulton Hall Methodist Primary School
- Morvant/Laventille Secondary School
- Penal Secondary School
- Pentecostal Light and Life High School
- Pleasantville Secondary School
- Point Fortin GVC
- Scarborough Secondary School
- Signal Hill Secondary School
- Sixth Form Government School
- List Of Tinidadian Speaking Engagements
- St. Anthony's College
- St James Secondary School
- Toco Secondary School
- Vessigny Secondary School

Universities/Higher Education:
- Ensafe: Institute for Health, Safety & Counseling

Training Ltd.

- Hugh Wooding Law School
- Laventille Open Bible School
- OASIS
- University of Trinidad and Tobago

Technical Institutes:

- HYPE O'Meara
- HYPE Sangre Grande
- HYPE St. Bede
- ICP Diego Martin
- MIC Laventille
- MUST Chagunanas
- MUST Laventille
- MIC Macoya
- MIC Tobago
- MUST Tunapuna
- MUST St. Madeline

Religious Establishments:

Catholic Churches:

- St. Ann's Roman Catholic Church

Seventh Day Adventist Churches:

- 3 Angels Ministry
- Longdenville
- Mary's Hill
- Mausica

List of Trinidadian Speaking Engagements

- San Juan
- Scarborough
- Wallerfield
- Methodist Churches:
- Belmont
- Fyzabad
- St. Madeline

Non-Denominational/Pentecostal Churches:

- Belle Garden Pentecostal Church
- Bible Way Temple
- Bride of Yeshua Messiah
- Calvary Road Deliverance Tabernacle
- Carnbee Gospel Hall
- Christ Crusaders Assembly
- Christian Fellowship Ministries
- Christian Union Church
- Church of the Nazarene
- Covenant House of Praise – Center of Excellence
- Deliverance Temple International
- Divine Encounter Fellowship Ministries International
- Faith Assembly International
- Faith In The Word
- Full Gospel Assemblies
- Guaico Pentecostal Church
- Holistic Transformation Ministries

- House of Mercy
- I-Care Christian Center
- Jesus Centered Outreach Ministry
- Lighthouse New Testament Church of God
- Light of Hope Ministries Training Centre
- Kingdom Global Advance
- Lowlands Lifeland
- Open Bible
- San Fernando Church of Christ
- Shiloh Pentecostal Tabernacle
- The 1 Movement
- The Apostles Ministries
- Upper Deliverance Room Tabernacle
- Urban Ministries Christian Center
- Woodbrook Pentecostal
- Word of Faith Gospel Tabernacle

Police Youth Clubs:

- Aripo
- Cashew Gardens
- Charlotteville
- Five Rivers
- Oropune
- Point Fortin
- Signal Hill
- St. Joseph

List of Trinidadian Speaking Engagements

Vacation Camps:

- Camp Swag
- Cadet Camp at San Juan North Secondary School
- Church of God of Prophecy
- Evangel Temple
- Five Rivers Nazarene Church
- Fyzabad
- The Kwami Ture Education Center
- Pan Camp
- Prizgar Lands Community Netball Team

Professional Establishments:

- Blue Waters Inn Hotel
- Colonial Life Insurance Company Ltd.
- Criminal Records Office
- Dolly and Associates Ltd.
- La Romaine Army Camp
- Ministry of National Security
- Nipdec
- Office of the Prime Minister
- Petrotrin
- Port of Spain Police Training Headquarters
- Servol
- St Mary's Children's Home

Community Meetings:

- Enid Village Miss Lynn Pre School – PTA Meeting
- Five Rivers Community Center

- Meteorology Building
- Moulton Hall Methodist Primary School – PTA Meeting
- PNM Party Group Seven Forum
- Point Fortin Community Meeting
- Rotary Club – Princes Town
- Scarborough Methodist Primary School
- Signal Hill Community Center
- The Human Equity Value Institute – City Women's Dialogue
- Woodbrook Secondary School – PTA Meeting

Public Libraries:

- Arima Library
- Maloney Library
- Sangre Grande Library
- Scarborough Public Library

Childhood Sexual Abuse

♦

Sexual violations are not discriminatory but are prevalent across every age, race, gender and culture; they are an equal opportunity employer as described by fellow U.S. attorney Gregory Love. They fall under four categories: Assault; harassment; sexual abuse; and peer abuse. Assault and harassment applies to adult to adult offences; sexual abuse refers to adult to child offences; whilst peer abuse involves child to child offences.

Often the misconception is that children are only abused by adults, typically a stranger; however, more disclosures have revealed the prevalence of peer to peer abuse especially involving siblings and other closely related family members.

Irrespective of the perpetrator's identity the sad reality is that we do not usually learn of the abuse until the victim becomes a survivor and shares their story some ten or twenty years later. The issue with disclosures of historic cases of abuse is often the absence of physical evidence; dozens more future victims; or the accused is deceased.

In many instances the child would have been groomed which often contributed to their silence, notwithstanding, the shame, guilt and embarrassment they would often feel after being subjected to inappropriate sexual invasions.

Every experience is not the same and it is therefore naïve for someone to make the assumption that the child was threatened into silence or that any dialogue took place. In some instances, no words are spoken which is most common when the child is sexually abused during their sleep.

It would be reasonable to assume that they would eventually be roused from their sleep by the physical contact, but often the child would pretend that he or she was still unconscious which was a 'game' of deception and protection they would 'play' with the accused who we could reasonably assume knew full well that the child was awake.

Grooming is one of the most effective ways that pedophiles prime their victims although it is a process that takes varying degrees of time and investment. It has not changed but merely advanced with the advent of technology.

Gender determines the way in which a child is groomed because boys and girls are wired differently. There is no disputing the fact that men and boys are visual and easily aroused while girls and women are emotional.

To groom a boy, they may be subjected to horseplay leading on to sexual touching; shown pornography;

given alcohol, marijuana or tobacco. The use of alcohol, pornography and marijuana all encourage secrecy. The alcohol and marijuana also impair judgment and are illegal, whilst the pornography stimulates arousal.

On the other hand, girls would require the building of a relationship which exhausts more time and effort, using mediums such as phones, Facebook, text messages, snap chat or other social media platforms. However, to groom a small child of either gender aged five this could include playful touch and isolation.

These actions would break down a child's defenses and typically distort their perception of the accused who they often love despite their violations. This does not make sense to the average individual who expects the victim to hate the accused but the best way to describe it would be that the child is 'conditioned.'

I had personally experienced a lot of insensitivity by some family members who claimed they understood, but then proceeded to ask me why I didn't scream, and why I didn't disclose that I was being abused at the time?

I was a victim of childhood sexual abuse by my mother's first husband between the ages of four to ten. It was attempted rape throughout those six fundamental developmental stages of my life. It therefore greatly shaped and impacted the way that I thought and perceived things as a young child.

Sexual abuse at such a young age taught me secrecy and how to compartmentalize and suppress my feelings. Even as an adult I have often had great difficulty identifying my feelings if they were anything other than 'happiness' or anger, the latter of which disguised rejection, abandonment, or sadness.

When insensitive people told survivors like me to move on because the abuse was in the past that did nothing but harbor the progress of our healing. It is therefore important for us to have the courage to remove ourselves from certain environments or even relationships to enable us to flourish.

In life there will always be people who will not understand or even more unhelpfully make comparisons with their own experience. Worse still there are people who say that they have moved on from their own sexual abuse experience but as I'd personally seen they had no friends; were controlling; demanding; selfish and had serious trust issues. In such instances I wish there was a manual, brochure or pamphlet that would explain to such so called 'survivor experts' that people do not just snap out of what they went through, or 'help themselves,' often they would need someone to help them, and there was usually a price tag attached to such help.

I finally began getting that help in Trinidad by not one but two therapists. For the first time in my young years I was asked more than, "How was your day?" but actually discussed the sexual abuse. Trinidad has been a lot of things and sadly my experiences had weighed heavily on the negative side, so it was amazing that at least one good thing had come out of the country.

After so many years had transpired since I first

received "It depends" to the question, "Can you keep a secret?" I was finally getting the help (albeit paid) I so desperately needed particularly at a time when my life was continuing to unfold in ways in which I could never have perceived or imagined.

I had fully claimed healing in Jesus' name but as a result of not receiving the help at a younger age in many ways I still suffered from the aftereffects of my childhood trauma. Insomnia was one of the issues I have struggled with my entire life. Being a victim of childhood sexual abuse does not define me, thus I frequently chose not to disclose something so personal to everyone that I met. I did not want sympathy or even a pity party and in my opinion most people would not even care because in their mind it had happened so long ago that it was simply time for me to move on.

This mindset was something I have personally witnessed time and time again from some of my family who could not see the 'physical' scars of my abuse, so naively assumed that they had somehow disappeared like magic. This made zero sense and was simply illogical but that was how they had chosen to think inadvertently making me feel guilty for not being 'fixed.' I was even once asked if I had depression which I found completely ludicrous since all I had were the 'indicators' of a person who'd been sexually abused as a child which was primarily lots of anger.

If you would take a moment to think about it, does that really come as a surprise? When someone who was supposed to care for you, sexually violated you, and the people who should have seen something and protected you did nothing, isn't anger a completely reasonable response and emotion? The alternative would be depression, bitterness and self-harm which are all 'internal,' and therefore much more destructive, whereas at least with anger it could be readily identified by others and thus treated.

The question would be whether people genuinely wanted to help a survivor get over their past abuse or simply sit back and impatiently wait for overnight results. The people in my life wanted quick results whilst they finger pointed, criticized, and cast judgment and comparisons at me. They treated me like the black sheep (pun intended) telling me that I was stigmatized and other such remarks to make me feel ashamed for sharing my story.

I do believe there is freedom in revelation and this book is a very public opportunity for me to open the door of my life in honesty and transparency because I am not ashamed of what was perpetrated upon me as an innocent child.

Sadly, there are people, who would not want to hear what I have to say, or even see my empowerment; instead they would be of the opinion that this is a Pandora's Box that should never have been opened. My former church included one such group of people many of whom shunned me after I publicly made my disclosure whilst making a request for prayer.

I would have never anticipated that the response I'd received would be so cold and judgmental. At the end of the day the church was the first place my disclosure needed to be heard and since it was God's house there could never be an inappropriate time to share a request for prayer. Furthermore, if reality really set in, the congregants should have begun to question why I was one of the 'older' young people who remained single when those who were much younger were already married with kids.

I guess it was one of those situations where the truth hurt especially since I grew up in that church and was very active there but not one person noticed the victim of abuse in their midst. I said what needed to be said and even went so far as protecting their reputation by lying and saying how much they had helped me when that had no ounce of truth. Individual congregants had blessed me tremendously, but the church as a whole had let me down.

It was therefore completely ludicrous that an insinuation had been made that I wanted attention and sympathy when making my disclosure at church because it had been a packed congregation. Far from it, the only thing I wanted was support and steadfast prayer for my healing and wholeness, so that I too could be married. Instead I received plenty of unwanted male attention from manipulative individuals old enough to be my father (who wanted to exploit the situation by) telling me how touched they were by the disclosure made by a 'beautiful attractive' individual Although I had begun life as a victim, I am astute enough and wise enough to see beyond the surface of a situation despite my insecurities and strong desire to be married. As imperfect as I am I remain open minded, I live as a survivor with a unique way of thinking and viewing things that is vastly different to that of many people, and although I still have a side of me that makes erroneous judgments, unlike many of my Christian counterparts I always do my best to view people through Jesus' lens (which includes those old men who were trying to pursue me).

Despite the remark I would sometimes make that my stepfather was dead and hopefully in hell, it may surprise you to know that I am a firm believer of second chances. Many people, Christian and non-Christian, would wholeheartedly disagree with me but they are entitled to their opinion, just as I am entitled to mine.

I read a story on Facebook of a man from Yemen whose wife died on their wedding night. When people heard about this case they were outraged calling him a murderer. Now I do not believe in murderers or rapists or pedophiles. I believe in human beings, human beings maybe with a tendency to rape, human beings with a tendency to murder, or human beings with a tendency to engage in sex with children.

As a Christian I believe that God sees everyone as human beings because, *"all have sinned, and come short of the glory of God."*[49] Consider for a moment that you stole $1 when you were a child, and no one ever found out about it, would that make you a thief? No, of course

---

[49] Romans 3:23 (KJV)

not, since you were never caught. But then what about the person who stole $1 and got caught, are they a thief? The unanimous response to that question would surely be, "Yes." I do not really get that because aren't both individuals thieves, regardless of whether they were caught and penalized?

As children, I believe that we have all made mistakes, done things we are not proud of, possibly even committed crimes. Let's say that every child had stolen at least once in their life e.g. a cookie, their mum's lipstick, their father's aftershave or $1. Our parents never found out and thus that criminal incident was overlooked and remained in the past. It is something we had no guilt over and did not even think about since it was such a minor event. What distinguishes us from someone who stole a cookie in a store, was caught, arrested and taken to jail? Why does that person get the label of thief, but we do not? I do not have an answer to that question it is just merely something for you to think about.

Now if I wanted to see change in Yemen, I would dress, eat and act like the people of Yemen without compromising my faith in Jesus Christ, and then I would say to Mr. Yemen, "Marriage is good, marriage is a beautiful thing, but your wife was six." When people became outraged by Mr. Yemen's marriage to a 6-year-old and her subsequent death on their wedding night I became confused, why? In my country, there are 40-year-old men having sex with 6-year- olds all the time who are not their wives.

Now please don't think I agree with 6-year-olds being married to 40-year-olds, far from it. However, at the end of the day, many of the things we are angered or disgusted by are the very same things taking place in our very own backyard - we just simply don't know about it, care about it, or turn a blind eye and make excuses for it. I believe that if we wanted change it should start with the way we think and the words that come out of our mouths.

The Bible says, *"Death and life are in the power of the tongue: and they that love it shall eat the fruit thereof."*[50] I believe that when you call someone a murderer that is all they can aspire to be. It is like a name; the name becomes who you are and defines you. I've seen this so often in my life; whenever I met a female with a certain name that individual proved[50] to be disingenuous, similarly whenever I've met a guy with a specific name they were often mischievous and a real headache for their parents. Did I shy away from people with those names? No, far from it because I always hoped that maybe they'd be different and not live up to their name; sadly, that has yet to be the case.

In the Philippines I spent some time with CICL (Children in Conflict with the Law) boys. I built a relationship with the children and loved them dearly. When I discovered the infractions that landed them in the rehabilitative children's home I was shocked. One of the older children had allegedly committed a

---

[50] Proverbs 18:21 (KJV)

114

serious crime, upon learning this I immediately judged him. This judgment lasted about 24-hours until I had a conversation with myself saying, "You have known this young adult for the last few weeks, he is polite, respectful, has a quiet countenance, is responsible and has been entrusted in the home. Why have you changed your opinion of him on the basis of some new information you've uncovered? Does that crime define who he is? No it doesn't because you have seen someone completely different."

I had a similar conversation with myself about two other children who were fluent in English (having self-taught themselves with the use of the dictionary and English movies). I loved the children as though they were my younger siblings. They were an absolute pleasure to be around. Once again, I had seen that their crimes did not define them.

Please understand I do not live with my head in the clouds, I 100% believe in jail to protect the victim and potential future victims. However, I also believe that all criminals have a right to a second chance at life. In the Bible there is a well-known scripture that says, *"For God so loved the world, that He gave His only begotten Son, that whosoever believeth in Him should not perish but have everlasting life."*[51] My understanding is that this invitation is for everyone and that although the Ten Commandments includes *"Thou shalt not kill"*[52] it does

---

[51] John 3:16 (KJV)

[52] Exodus 20:13 (KJV)

not have a caveat … do not kill except for Peter Scully,[53] do not kill except for Hitler.

In my opinion who are we to judge? I will never excuse the sick behavior perpetuated by Peter Scully, however I wholeheartedly believe that Jesus died for him too. I also believe that with the power of God, Peter Scully could change but I am in no way disillusioned that someday he would because it really isn't that simple. At the end of the day, if God could speak the earth into existence,[54] it really wouldn't be too difficult for Him to change the heart and mind of an individual like Scully.

Whenever I heard comments like, "There are people who have committed such terrible crimes and deserve the death penalty," it was a statement that I wholly disagreed with because who made us judge? What was considered to be a heinous crime by one person might not be perceived as heinous to another. Plus, for all we knew Peter Scully was a victim of the same abuse that he perpetrated against many defenseless and innocent Filipino children. On the other hand, maybe that is very far from the truth but there have been occasions when people who had been abused went on to commit those very same acts that were previously inflicted upon them. In such an instance does that make the person evil or does it make them a victim too?

---

[53] Candace Sutton, "Rot In Hell", *The Sun*, June 14, 2018. https://www.thesun. co.uk/news/6525841/peter-scully-worlds-worst-paedophile-jail-baby- rape-dig-graves-philippines/

[54] Genesis 1 (KJV)

The Bible says that we have all *"come short of the Glory of God"*.[55] People are people and we all make mistakes, some 'mistakes' are intentional and calculated, while others are genuine accidents. I hold the firm belief that your past does not have to dictate your future; you do not have to be defined by your culture; your upbringing; or by the friends and family around you, instead you can choose your identity. My identity is not in my accomplishments, it is in who God describes me as, in Psalm 139, *"I am fearfully and wonderfully made;.... You knit me together in my mother's womb."*[56]

There have been many people in the world who believed that their life was not an accident, but that there was a purpose for them on the earth. Sadly, many of those very same people had never discovered their purpose because something held them back, be it fear, circumstance, familial influence etc.

A number of high school students asked me what they should study to become a lawyer and likewise an older single guy sought me out for advice. He wanted to meet me to have a conversation about becoming a lawyer because that was allegedly his dream. Now, I am certainly not as naïve as some people perceive me to be, so I told him rather assertively that I was an unpaid lawyer, so clearly not the best person to give him career advice. In my opinion if he was really sincere about learning from me, he would not have been deterred by

---

[55] *Supra* 45

[56] Psalm 139:13-14 (NIV)

my rejection of an in-person meeting but instead would have opted to speak by telephone.

That sort of thing was what I considered to be a decoy which I have never fallen for in the past. Sadly, my physical appearance and single status often gave desperate men the wrong idea that they had a chance with me. They did not; despite the frequent joke I made about looking for a young, hot Christian single guy to marry; News Flash: It was only a joke! As I would frequently say, "I'm not desperate. If I was I'd be in a relationship or married already."

The experiences I've had are too numerous to list, the common theme throughout was that I simply wasn't interested which I always made explicitly clear. I've had men message me with their so-called problems and once I said, "I'm unable to help or provide them free legal advice," they'd ask if I wanted to hang out. I have truly reached the point where I am sick to death of guys asking me to hang out; the answer is unequivocally "NO!" That was why I felt like a complete hypocrite when I asked a new acquaintance to hang out, it was actually one of the hardest things I'd ever done before, even more so because I actually didn't have any intention of hanging out but just felt strongly that it was a request I needed to make.

One guy came up to me after my presentation at his church and shared his story of being sexually abused. At first I didn't know it was him because he had lied and said that it was a friend but when he finally confided in me that he was the victim he then proceeded to give me a play by play detailed account of what had transpired between him and the accused. I don't remember if I had taken a big gulp as he shared his story, but I had felt incredibly uncomfortable as we stood at the front of the church with what felt like one sided 'phone' sex. I honestly did not know what to do but I strongly believed he was trying but failing to groom me.

Another guy I met during my first trip to Trinidad began talking to me outside Movietowne where I was with some friends. Despite the unwritten rule that I should never be unaccompanied they separated from me leaving me alone with a complete stranger. When we made introductions, he told me that he had heard my accent hence the reason he followed me. We started talking and he explained that he was a school sports coach. He then told me that he had a student sexually abused at age five and age ten and that at sixteen she was a lesbian. He then quite nonchalantly said that he had a video. At the time I was completely clueless until I had one of those light bulb moments. It was a pornographic video of his 16-year-old student that he had wanted me to see.

Now, whenever I have discussed this experience with my audience, the adults in the room usually believed that the sports coach wanted me to see the video because I am a lawyer. Wrong! Outside of the police station with my client it would be a crime for me to watch child pornography and I do not work with pedophiles knowingly, (but of course I've worked with pedophiles I just didn't know it). When I discussed this incident at a boys' high school they were rather explicit in explaining that the man wanted to groom me for sex.

A while later the sports coach messaged me on WhatsApp saying, "When I first met you and said it was your accent, I lied. I want to follow my interior." Now when I initially read that I mistakenly thought it was a Trinidad term because where I come from we would say, "I want to follow my heart, I want to follow my passions," or maybe "I want to follow my hormones," (after marriage of course), but I had never heard that one before. I was again presenting at a boys' high school when one of the students shouted out, "Miss, it's like that cookie story, 'Daddy is eating my cookie.'" E.g. Cookie a.k.a interior a.k.a male genitals. I subsequently never spoke to the sports coach again and promptly blocked him on WhatsApp.

Anyway, back to what I was saying earlier about being asked for career advice. Honestly, I did not have any because my journey to law was so unconventional. Therefore, whenever I have been asked, my reply has always been, "It doesn't matter what you study. It only counts when you study for your degree. So, choose whatever subject you enjoy."

That's exactly what I did! I left school at fifteen with D and E grades. Since I was in the foundation tier D and E grades were the highest I could achieve. I then studied four years of cooking, two years in England at two different colleges, and then two years in Switzerland. Then in my final year abroad I did an internship as a chef at the United Nations in Geneva.

Prior to the completion of my second year at the Institute Hotelier Cesar Ritz, I read 'Point of Origin' by Patricia Cromwell. That book changed my life and was the pivotal moment when I decided I wanted to quit my current studies and be a C.S.I. – Crime Scene Investigator. I was a huge C.S.I. Vegas fan at the time and wanted to walk around with a gun among handsome men while dusting for fingerprints. Thank God I took the advice of my mum, to complete what I had started. Despite my new- found study path, I obeyed, and I am glad that I did because at the end of those two years I graduated with an International Diploma in Hotel Management. The alternative would have been an incomplete period of study that would not have looked very impressive on my resume.

After completing my diploma, I returned to England where I relocated to the North East to study an access year of mathematics and science at Teesside University. Despite my previous start in life I attained an A in mathematics. How? I had always been an A student because I had been privately tutored throughout high school. During that year I also studied criminal law and forensic science. I loved criminal law but was bored with the forensics since dusting for fingerprints wasn't all it was cut out to be, not to mention the absence of handsome men.

The following year I studied police studies with the desire to become a police officer. It too was boring, so during the first week of my second year I decided to pursue a degree in law. People have always asked me, why did I choose law? It was a truly presumptive question because I did not choose it, it chose me. As my family would strongly attest I am argumentative by nature. But aside from that one obvious fact, I believe that I was born to be a lawyer. I think like a lawyer and one of my greatest gifts besides my observational skills is that I have the gift of the gab. I can make things up on the spot that sound convincing.

Unfortunately, there have been a number of literal people who misunderstood that statement as meaning I fabricated information, so let me explain as best as I can in layman's terms. I have acquired knowledge on human trafficking, child abuse and exploitation through reading books and other material, watching documentaries, attending presentations and independent research. Whenever I have been invited on the T.V. or radio I was always 99.9% unprepared.

Despite arriving between one to three hours early, I have usually only had a few seconds with the interviewer beforehand to inform them of the topics I'd like to discuss, the name of my organization, website and contact details. Having watched myself back on countless interviews I have always been truly amazed by the results. Often whilst live on air I would begin analyzing how I'd answered a particular question; and sometimes I would be over thinking so much that I was not paying attention to what was actually being asked but somehow still managing to answer the next question with a great deal of confidence; fluency and eloquence.

It is truly a gift from God, there is no other way for me to describe it. Having been publicly speaking for only about a total of eleven weeks at the time of writing, it was a small miracle that I came across so poised, with 100% absence of "Erms....You know...and." Whenever I would listen to others on the program after me I would count the number of "Erms". Please understand I did not do this because I thought I was somehow better than them, far from it, in fact usually they would have years more knowledge and experience than I had on whatever subject they were sharing about.

As the Bible says *"But God hath chosen the foolish things of the world to confound the wise;"*[57] which has totally been my experience. I was completely in new territory but somehow I had the confidence of someone who was very comfortable being in the public domain. I did find it really amusing however, that whenever I got off air I would "Erm," and "You know," which really goes to show that it wasn't some natural gifting or talent that I had, but was simply a God thing.

I have had the privilege of talking to audiences of up to eight hundred around the world on human trafficking, child sexual abuse, incest, pornography and prostitution. It has always been a learning experience and not just for my audience but also for me.

Unlike presenters before me who would share solely on human trafficking I would take my audience on

---

[57] 1 Corinthians 1:27 (KJV)

a journey beginning with the sexual abuse of a child aged five and the effects of childhood trauma. Sexual abuse is still such a taboo subject that it is often not discussed but instead swept under the carpet. I believe that 99% of parents educate their children about their body parts and that they should not be touched but sadly, in my opinion this was not enough. Furthermore, being uncomfortable talking about sex and abuse would never safeguard children; instead it would be the equivalent of closing your eyes and hoping that it was not really happening.

The Catholic Church has had a reputation for doing exactly that, hiding disclosures of sexual abuse and protecting the priests. This has happened so frequently that the Catholic Church has a long-standing reputation of housing and hiding pedophiles which although frequently true, they have not been the only denomination or faith group to do so.

In America I was told the story of a group of girls who were brought inside the Christian Bible study for sex, not the Catholic Bible study. I also heard about a boy that was raped in the basement of his church during scout meeting. That church was not Catholic. I also met a survivor of sexual abuse who shared that he had been sexually abused in nursery during the prayer meeting. Aside from the fact that it was not the Catholic prayer meeting, what confused me most about that last story was how exactly it had happened as I know for a fact that people sometimes have their eyes open during prayer meetings.

I have sadly heard countless other stories of rape and abuse by pastors who were not from the Catholic faith. One such story was of historic childhood sexual abuse and the accused was still the pastor of his church. The survivor of abuse reached out to me and asked if I could present at her former pastor's church. I agreed and asked my personal assistant (P.A.) to call him. My P.A. called and called but to no avail, however, the pastor eventually text her back saying he would be in touch soon.

Since I am a born again Christian and pray to Jesus Christ directly I asked my friends around the world to join me in praying because I wanted to present at the pedophile pastor's church on Sunday. On Monday we prayed. On Tuesday, he died.

I don't know what they prayed, but he died on Tuesday. Now imagine if that pastor was still alive and I had indeed presented at his church, he may have said to me, "That was such a good presentation, especially about pedophile pastors."

In other words, who is in your world? Who is sitting right next to you (figuratively speaking of course)?

No matter how much parents try their best to protect their children, how far will that protection go if the church pastor or a biological family member is a pedophile? Paranoia never helped anyone, but wisdom certainly did. As society has been learning it is not just stepfathers that abuse but also biological fathers, grandfathers, cousins, mothers, sisters and aunties.

I read a Facebook post once that completely traumatized me. It was about a couple who I believe were African American. At the age of sixteen the girl began to develop feelings of attraction towards the other person but decided to wait until she was eighteen before engaging in sex with them. At eighteen they then began having sex. The person she was having sex with was her mother. The part of the article that really messed with my head was when the daughter had said, "Me and my mum do mums and daughter things, but we enjoy having sex together."

In my mind that was completely sick; I believed that the mother was a pedophile who had a sexual attraction towards her child who she groomed into becoming her lover. I wondered if when the child was 5-years-old the mother had kissed her on the lips and engaged in inappropriate sexual touching. When I shared this article on Facebook, someone I knew commented, "Well if it makes them happy." Such a response raised alarm bells in my mind and my immediate reaction was not to formulate any kind of friendship with that individual. As I would often say to my audience, "Just because something is legal, does not make it right," and at the time of reading that article incest was not yet legal in the U.S.

So, what exactly is sexual abuse? It includes:

- Inappropriate touching of the child's genitals
- This could be used as a form of sexual grooming and is sometimes how the abuse begins with touching over and then under the child's clothing.

- Engaging the child in sexual activity with another child or adult[58]
- Taking sexually explicit photos of the child
- Exposing a child to watch or listen to sex
- "Inappropriately watching a child undress or use the bathroom"[59]
- Rape, which is sex
- Attempted rape, which is NOT sex
- Showing pornography to a child
- Standing naked in front of a child.

This list is not exhaustive and can be categorized into touching and non-touching categories. The example that my audience consistently had a hard time accepting was the last point, particularly because it was something that was so frequently done in Trinidad and Tobago often without any malicious intent.

Standing naked in front of a child constitutes indecent exposure, it also sensitizes or desensitizes that child to an adult's nudity. Although that parent's intent might not have been sexually deviant, when that child would venture next door and the pedophile neighbor was also naked, the child would think nothing of it because that behavior had become normalized.

Whenever I would share this to my audience I would always get mixed responses. Often there would be

---

[58] Parents Protect!, "What Is Child Sexual Abuse", Accessed August 25, 2018. https://www.parentsprotect.co.uk/what-is-child-sexual-abuse.htm

[59] *Ibid*

a few nods of agreements but more frequently there were individuals who were deeply challenged by this revelation and in complete disagreement with me even going so far as to call me crazy and how it was a good thing I did not have children of my own. As someone once said, "There will always be people who will disagree with your presentation but that's because either they are or were a victim or they are doing or have done the victimizing. The truth hurts." By the grace of God from the time I first began presenting I have only ever received positive reviews including multiple invitations to speak again.

I personally do not see what there is to agree or disagree about. I am an attorney, so I would usually speak from a legal perspective but in layman's terms. I have always spoken facts from either firsthand experience or exposure and I would often share my own personal opinion. Each of these would be separate and aside from one another and I have always made it clear which one of the three I was sharing.

As one audience member explained, "Standing naked in front of a child is like pornography." I wholeheartedly agreed because by phrasing it that way, it makes a lot more sense since pornography was imagery whether fixed or moving depicting nudity, sexual activity or the exposure of genitals.

A question I began asking my audience was whether or not they had been exposed to pornography. To avoid confusion, I placed emphasis on certain words and would repeat the question twice. Interestingly when I asked this once at a church the pastor's hand was prostrate, and when I asked this at the Office of the Prime Minister a mature lady in the audience (who I believed to be a devote Christian), was completely flabbergasted by the question and of course had her hand held high.

Whenever someone would raise their hand to that question I would then proceed by asking them if they owned a T.V. or used the internet, following which their hand would always promptly come down. Whenever I would ask this question if my audience were truly honest all hands would be down because in my opinion we have all been exposed to pornography. Game of Thrones, Cosmopolitan magazine, 50 Shades of Grey, Amazon, YouTube, VMA Awards, Music videos and of course the internet have often been the cause of our exposure.

I was told the story of a boy aged ten who had been caught raping a female peer. When the police arrested and interviewed him they asked, "When you were raping that girl and she cried and said no, why didn't you stop?" To which he replied, "I see that in pornography, women cry and say no." In other words, 'no,' did not mean no anymore.

I also know of a woman married to her second husband, whose first husband made pornography with her without her consent. That pornography is still being sold on the internet today; therefore not all pornography is consensual. Furthermore, not all pornography is found on the XXX channel but sometimes right inside a child's bedroom on their video game consul.

Games like Grand Theft Auto V sensitize its players to the idea that women and girls are merely a commodity to be used for the sexual pleasure of men and boys. I have never played it myself, but I was informed by teenage boys in Trinidad and in Ghana that you pick up a prostituted individual who performs a sex act on you. You then pay her $50.00, beat her up, murder her and get your money back. Believing this game is just mere entertainment is simply foolish, it is desensitization.

I have never been one for video games as a child so my exposure to pornography came through the internet. During the days of dial up I would get pop up ads and receive e-mails from women who thought I was male and would solicit me with offers of sexual services. Even Facebook exposed me to pornography when I received a friend request with a profile picture of a woman performing a sex act on a man.

The reality is that no matter how much we might try to protect and guard ourselves; vices like pornography will often still find a way to creep in. Children are a lot less innocent now than were in the 70s and 80s and modern technology has a lot to do with that. Nowadays when we talk about sexual abuse the perpetrator could be on the other side of the world sitting in front of his/her electronic device or they could be a lot closer to home and be a peer of the victim. Anyone could be a victim of childhood sexual abuse and knowing what signs to look out for is the first step in identifying an abusive situation to enable that child to get the help and protection that they need.

Safeguarding Against Childhood Sexual Abuse

◆

T he most effective way to protect children from sexual abuse would be by engaging in age appropriate communication throughout all stages of their upbringing.

Children are becoming exposed to sexual activity at a young age and consequently their knowledge and understanding is often surprising. I have been frequently educated by children aged seven, eight and nine who all gave better definitions of a pimp than the average adult. Children would quite often see things that adults did not because most adults would make excuses for inappropriate behavior or unknowingly give the perpetrator the benefit of the doubt.

It is therefore important to listen to children irrespective of their age and communication level. Babies and toddlers should never be forced to kiss, hug or sit on the lap of friends or family members. But instead they should be taught that they have the right over their body and can respectfully say "No." When considering the reality that incest abuse is so prevalent this is really fundamental.

Very young children usually indicate immediately if they are uncomfortable with something and once they develop the ability to talk they often vocalize that information. There are always exceptions to the rule however, but body language and eye contact are also a great indicator.

In child appropriate environments such as schools, nurseries and churches a literal fence of some form is usually erected to safeguard the children. The problem with the 'fence' is that its structure relates to keeping the threat out, but rarely considers that it may be keeping the threat in. Numerous cases in the media have identified this fact with frequent reports about camp counselors, youth leaders, ministers, teachers and gym instructors sexually abusing children under their authority and care.

Our belief system dictates the decisions that we make which are sometimes harmful or hazardous. When considering suitable child care for your children you may unknowingly place them in a situation that makes them vulnerable to sexual abuse; or even make comments that could be manipulated by a perpetrator to their advantage.

An example of this could be with a baby sitter, nanny or even an older sibling that is responsible for another child e.g. putting them to bed or looking after them during the day. A parent could very innocently tell their child, "Tonight your brother (the nanny, or baby sitter) is going to look after you whilst I've gone out. Make sure that you do everything that she/he says."

Without meaning to, the above statement has given the responsible individual (i.e. the brother, nanny or baby sitter) complete authority over the child, and the child must obey every instruction.

Instead it would be better to say something like, "Tonight your brother (the nanny or baby sitter) is going to look after you, and you know the rules. You must not do anything that you are uncomfortable with, or that you cannot discuss with me."

This isn't a script but merely a suggestion of how you can more appropriately word your instructions to your child when they are going to be cared for by someone else.

Of course, the second most important thing to do is to have a conversation with your child the next day to discuss what happened, placing great emphasis on whether they experienced anything uncomfortable. Your reaction to the child's response is crucial because if something did happen and they initially deny it, if you respond with relief they may decide not to tell you. Similarly, understanding the likelihood of a denial requires you to leave the conversation open by encouraging the child that they can talk to you at any time if they did experience something that they were uncomfortable with, and of course letting them know that anything that may have happened to them was not their fault.

It is important to acknowledge however, that female disclosures of abuse are more prevalent than male disclosures which are evident by the #metoo movement as well as reports in the media. Boys are just as likely to become victims of sexual abuse as girls and having read hundreds of articles detailing child pornography involving boys I know that this is indeed a reality.

Even from my own experience having met dozens of women and girls who disclosed historic cases of sexual abuse, the number of men and boys to date has been less than a handful. Generally speaking, men and boys do not share if they've been abused even more so if the abuser was male.

The shame, stigma and embarrassment they often felt, coupled with doubts about their sexuality and masculinity would in some way explain their silence. However, regardless of gender, making a disclosure of sexual abuse is often a very frightening experience whether or not the child had been threatened into silence. Breaking that silence takes a great deal of courage that the average person simply cannot understand. As a child, formulating into words the violation that they have experienced is incredibly difficult, even more so when they have never engaged in talks of a sexual nature.

Even when that child becomes adolescent, being educated about sex is usually shied away from by parents and left up to the school teachers. Consequently, since sex is often such a taboo subject at home it is therefore no surprise that a conversation about sexual abuse is often incredibly difficult.

It has often surprised me however, that children in the West would talk so freely amongst their peers about the sexual activity they 'consensually' engaged in but would be seen to shut down completely when the subject turned to a much more personal nature, namely abuse.

A lot of fear, much of which is imagined silences a lot of victims. The greatest fears usually concerned being disbelieved; being accused of making things up or having brought the situation upon themselves.

Any individual could be sexually abused, and any individual could be an abuser. Abuse has not only been perpetrated by the stereotypical strange male, but could include doctors, lawyers, teachers, gym instructors, judges, policemen, and pastors.

Sexual abuse has become increasingly rampant in today's society especially in churches. The majority of people have their guard down and depending upon the church community, the attendees would typically form fast relationships, becoming very over familiar with one another much more than in most environments. Despite popular belief it is my strong opinion that Catholic priests are not pedophiles; but instead that there are people who are pedophiles who sometimes happen to be Catholic priests.

Although I have been critiqued for not discussing pedophilic Catholic priests in this book I do not feel there is any justifiable need to do so because in my opinion it is old news. In other words, since everyone is talking about sexual abuse in the Catholic Church I chose to talk about something different. When everyone was focused on Catholicism they were forgetting about the child marriage and sexual abuse that took place in the fundamentalist Mormon Church, and the frequent stories we heard involving pastors and parishioners in Pentecostal churches.

I have even heard firsthand accounts of sexual abuse in the Seventh Day Adventist Church and a number of other Christian and non-Christian denominations in the Philippines and Trinidad. Once again I want to reiterate the point that I made earlier, people are people. If the world considered this fact for a moment nothing would surprise them, instead the words we often hear are, "I would never have suspected…" Why is that? Often the person we would least expect looks just like us, after all it is typically the people closest to us who violate the children in our world because our guard is down.

Perpetrators are looking for easy access and availability which is why they will often seek out certain types of employment giving them unmerited access to children. Therefore a safety system and appropriate policy should be established to effectively protect the children.

Training must be paramount for anyone in an environment with children, not merely those with direct contact. In a school environment for example the janitor or security guard may observe inappropriate behavior therefore it is equally important that they too receive the appropriate training. Each employee is an integral part of the work environment and should be treated as such while also empowering them to report information on something that they might have seen. It is important that inappropriate behavior is identified as such, which would only be possible if everyone has the same understanding of what is and is not appropriate. Cultural differences and upbringing would mean that a hug may be deemed appropriate by one individual, whilst deemed inappropriate by another. I have personally experienced this throughout my travels when I witnessed physical contact between staff and children (of the same gender) which included hugging, holding hands and even massages.

The hugging and holding hands appeared innocent, however, because of the strict no contact laws in England and the U.S. I found the behavior strange. The massages, however, were something that I had huge fault with and continue to do so. Some may say that this is because I grew up in a country with heavy child protection legislation; however, I feel that it has much more to do with the sexualized connotations of massages especially in a country like the Philippines.

To my knowledge I have not witnessed massages being 'misused,' and it was only between females but in my opinion it simply was not right. Furthermore, the children were in a home where they were being cared for, having them perform massages on the staff could constitute child labor and exploitation.

I believe that the Filipino staff who engaged in such behavior would have vehemently disagreed with my sentiments on this issue; therefore, it is understandably crucial that everyone is on the same page as to what constitutes inappropriate behavior. Then if such behavior is observed there is an appropriate reporting procedure in place, because too often than not, staff did not know who to bring such concerns too and would often remain silent on the issue.

In church environments however, when the information was reported, the response was often that it was a Matthew 18[60] situation and that any further discussion of the matter constituted gossip. This is probably why the Catholic Church have been under so much fire, because for far too long, allegations of abuse were swept under the carpet, with the accused retaining his or her position and of course unmerited access to potential future victims.

Understandably the church would want to protect its reputation, but there is simply no justification for inaction at the expense of harming countless victims. As the Bible rightly says, "What is done in the dark comes out in the light."[61]

The Catholic Church has failed on many counts, most of all the inability to appreciate that the best predictor of future behavior is past behavior.

---

[60] *"If your brother or sister sins, go and point out their fault, just between the two of you. If they listen to you, you have won them over. But if they will not listen, take one or two others along, so that 'every matter may be established by the testimony of two or three witnesses.' If they still refuse to listen, tell it to the church; and if they refuse to listen even to the church, treat them as you would a pagan or a tax collector."* Matthew 18:15-17 (NIV)

[61] *"For there is nothing hidden that will not be disclosed, and nothing concealed that will not be known or brought out into the open."* Luke 8:17 (NIV)

But when does pedophilic behavior actually begin? The statistics vary, and their veracity has to be measured against the disclosure from the accused, but the reality is that the vast majority of those accused have never entered the criminal justice system and consequently walk undetected among us. On the other hand, those who are in the system may indeed lie because they might be too ashamed to detail the full extent of their crime or perverse sexual behavior. Either of these individuals fits into one of two categories, abduction offender or preferential offender.

The abduction offender is often widely discussed amongst parents and children with warnings of stranger danger. They, however, make up a smaller percentage of the problem because they are opportunist criminals with no connection to the child.

Preferential offenders are the greater issue because not only are they 'inside the fence' but they are least likely to be suspected because the fixation is on an outside abuser coming inside. Their preference is often towards a child sexual partner of a specific gender and/or age. Some of these individuals may have had a desire towards one child which we would sometimes read about when a teacher was caught engaging in sex with a single student.

A number of years ago a High Court Judge that I shadowed made the comment that some individuals were pedophiles who had an attraction towards children, whereas others were not because their attraction had been to one child. At first I did not understand his statement but over time it began to make sense. I would not go so far as to say that I agree with his point, but I understood what he had been conveying.

About seven or so years ago I followed a case of a student who ran away with her teacher. In applying the judge's point, we would assume that the teacher was not a pedophile but had developed romantic feelings for one of his students who he began a relationship with. I in no way condone that relationship however; I believe that the teacher did not love his student but that this had simply been about sex and the abuse of power. Why do I say that?

One word, patience! 1 Corinthians 13 says, *"Love is patient."*[62] This is one of the most important messages I have tried educating young people about because often their lack of understanding about love is the reason why they were pressured into having sex prematurely when their boyfriend or girlfriend said, "If you love me, have sex with me."

If that teacher had really loved his student, he would have waited until she turned sixteen, instead he engaged in sex with a minor for which he was imprisoned. In my opinion, if he loved her he would not have wanted to be separated by a prison sentence, and thus would have waited until the law would permit their relationship.

---

[62] 1 Corinthians 13:4-8 (NIV)

In this case and many others inappropriate behavior is often identified but then excused away.

Appropriate screening should be undertaken for all new applicants, including criminal background checks and references. Emphasis should never be placed solely upon background checks which excludes those individuals who have gone undetected which far often than not tends to be the majority of perpetrators. When considering the fact that sexual abuse often went unreported for years or even decades it becomes evident that little weight can be given to a 'clear' background check.

Instead further digging should be undertaken namely through obtaining information from referees, particularly by asking questions that would highlight high risk identifiers. This level of screening should not be limited to fitness for purpose and suitability for the job but instead consider the safety of children in the care, supervision or vicinity of that individual.

Those individuals with a predatory nature towards children can effectively groom the gatekeeper and acquire the job. Even the use of a probationary period fails to act as a deterrent because they will often excel allowing them to get one step closer to accessing the children.

Sexual abuse prevention training should be mandatory for all current and future employees inside any establishment with children. It should be conducted in an innovative way to ensure that the information is retained, and consequently refresher courses should be frequently given.

The initial training should encompass the procedures that are in place to protect children from abuse from both inside and outside of the facility. The next thing to establish would be that everyone has the same understanding of what constitutes sexual abuse whether physical, verbal or visual. This provides an opportunity to dispel the myth that sexual abuse requires contact because non-contact activity can also constitute a crime.

In doing so this training would serve as an effective deterrent prior to hiring as it would enable the perpetrator to 'self-select out.' By ensuring that all employees have received training on sexual abuse, the perpetrator would develop the realization that everyone is on the same page and therefore on the lookout for any inappropriate behavior. He or she would have the foresight to decline the position knowing that their planned intentions would not go unnoticed.

Being overly protective of a child can often do more harm than good, and paranoia is not particularly helpful. Fear creates two groups of people, the fearful and the fearless. The former were usually the most enthusiastic at my presentations and felt that the information I had given them somehow validated their overprotective behavior. The fearless were those who would not attend my presentation (unless under duress) because they believed sexual abuse would never come knocking at their door.

Both groups were at extreme ends of the scale and therefore required a balance since neither over protectiveness nor under protectiveness could be considered wise. Instead, taking proactive steps such as these safeguarding tips are highly effective at minimizing the risk of sexual abuse.

What's Your Currency?

◆

Whilst participating in the Ask Why? Television program discussion, fellow panelist Alloy Youk See used the term 'currency' in reference to grooming by traffickers.

Currency is defined as:

1. "A system of money in general use in a particular country.

2. The fact or quality of being generally accepted or in use.

3. The time during which something is in use or operation."[63]

I have since borrowed the term 'currency' to help victims and survivors of abuse, as well as the general public better understand their vulnerability so as to prevent potential future exploitation.

Young and old, males and females of all ethnicities have one primary thing in common, needs. This, however, is where the commonality starts and ends because unlike

---

[63] Oxford University Press, *"Oxford Dictionaries"*, Accessed August 30, 2018. https://en.oxforddictionaries.com/definition/currency

popular opinion I do not believe that we can lump all human beings together as having a male or female need which has been commonly described as a man's need for sex and a woman's need for an empathetic listener. Instead I believe that our needs are uniquely different.

If we refer back to the Garden of Eden, we would recall that Eve engaged in deep conversation with a snake[64] which led to her downfall. Adam on the other hand, saw a naked Eve and subsequently fell into sin.[65] From the beginning of creation we would garner that women are tempted by what they hear and men by what they see. It is therefore no wonder that men and boys would often whisper sweet nothings to a woman or use the line, "If you love me you would have sex with me," to get what they wanted.

Contrary to popular belief however, the first sin was not indeed sex, because the Bible does not shy away from the use of that word but instead makes frequent references to sex and fornication throughout. Instead that story in Genesis 3 makes reference to the weakness of men and women.

---

[64] *"Now the serpent was more crafty than any of the wild animals the Lord God had made. He said to the woman, "Did God really say, 'You must not eat from any tree in the garden'?" The woman said to the serpent, "We may eat fruit from the trees in the garden, but God did say, 'You must not eat fruit from the tree that is in the middle of the garden, and you must not touch it, or you will die.'" "You will not certainly die," the serpent said to the woman. "For God knows that when you eat from it your eyes will be opened, and you will be like God, knowing good and evil." Genesis 3:1-5*

[65] *"When the woman saw that the fruit of the tree was good for food and pleasing to the eye, and also desirable for gaining wisdom, she took some and ate it. She also gave some to her husband, who was with her, and he ate it. Then the eyes of both of them were opened, and they realized they were naked; so they sewed fig leaves together and made coverings for themselves." Genesis 3:6-7*

It is important to note however, that not all men are tempted visually, nor is every woman tempted by what she hears. This may be hard for some people to believe because it often seems that the majority of males and females respond in this way.

I personally have not been tempted by words of seduction or affirmation. Although I thrive from being encouraged and praised, such language would be ineffective in getting me into a guy's bed, no matter how much he tried. Why? For one thing I am not wired that way; most likely I would not believe what was being said (even if it was true), plus I know manipulation when I see it.

Sad to say there are a lot of women and girls who because of insecurity feed off men's words to their peril. It is very heartbreaking to see and hear their stories of being used as a plaything, at the disposal of different men. Sadder still is that these girls have often been deceived into believing that the guy loves them when this was very far from the truth. Usually the guy 'loves' what the girl has to offer, that is until someone else comes along.

Many of us wear our currency on our sleeve; therefore, it would not take someone very long to assess our vulnerability. The way that we dress, walk, behave and carry ourselves speaks much more than the words coming out of our mouths, and often no matter how much we would fake it, our real persona is easily revealed.

Consider observing an individual in the Philippines who looks, dresses and acts like a man, and has an immense hatred for men. Unbeknownst to you at first glance, the individual is in fact female. The question you might have besides, "What is their currency?" is the dynamics behind the way they present themselves. Or, how about a very loud mouthed, aggressive and overly intimidating female who frequently uses profanity and has a tendency towards physical violence. What would her currency be?

Both individuals are female and Filipino, but they are polar opposites of each other. The first one, in this example, is a lesbian and thus the sweet whispers of a man would be in vain. The second is a heterosexual with a difficult past.

Their currency would be arguably different. With the lesbian she would have been looking for acceptance of her sexuality and choice of lifestyle, whilst the aggressor would be looking for love, but had built a hard exterior as protection from being hurt.

In the latter instance, the aggressor had suffered past abuse and violations which she may or may not have appropriately dealt with. Consequently, as a result of a mix of betrayal and un-forgiveness she unintentionally pushed people away in an attempt at safeguarding herself. The result, however, would be that she had been left feeling very empty and lonely because people were intimidated and frightened by her.

Someone who could exhibit immense patience, and withstand the vulgar language, would be able to

148

infiltrate past the firm exterior and eventually take control of her by using the currency of love. This would not have to be romantic love, since such a person would usually have few genuine friends but rather people that tolerated her behavior; and she would often be of the belief that the whole world was against her.

Bearing all of this in mind, if a pimp exercised sufficient patience he would eventually gain the trust of this woman and get her to adhere to his whims without her even realizing. That reality is actually very scary, however it is not my desire to create fear but to share knowledge and wisdom.

With boys and men, generally speaking, we could make the statement that they need a father figure in their life, and thus growing up in a single female parent household affects the decisions they will make later in life such as preen teen sexual activity and joining gangs. This has of course not always been the case, and there are always exceptions to the rule, however, it is something that has been seen with great frequency.

On the other hand, with girls growing up in a single female parent household the effects are vastly different with the girl shying away from joining a gang but instead having a romantic relationship with an older man which often simulated the missing father figure.

Bearing this in mind, I am concerned about how children would be affected if they grew up with two dads or two mums, since what has usually been the case is that the average child grew up with their mother. My fear is that since girls who grew up without a father usually end up dating a much, much older guy. If, they instead grew up with two dads and no mother, would they later go on to date an older woman since the mother figure was absent? I really do not have the answers, but it has been something I have often thought about because whether we choose to accept it or not, decisions parents make either positively or negatively affect their children.

Now, I want you to consider for a moment being the teenage son or daughter of a famous musician. You live in a beautiful home, are driven in beautiful cars and have a life of luxury. Both parents tour together, leaving you home alone with only the house help, gardener and security detail as company. In a situation such as this your 'currency' would be the attention and companionship of your parents.

Bearing this in mind, is it any wonder that the children of some celebrities shoplift, drive under the influence of drugs and/or alcohol, and land themselves in jail? Besides the publicity that would follow when the media splash this all over the papers, what would usually happen was that the parents would bail them out as a sign of solidarity and support for their wayward child.

The average layman would usually be perplexed by such destructive behavior, even more so the shoplifting since the child could afford the items in question. My theory is that the child wanted their busy parent's attention and found that a run in with the law was the most effective means of doing so.

Let's consider a scenario that's much closer to home, using myself as an example. To give a bit of background,

What's Your Currency?

I was an only child that grew up with my mother and stepfather. My mother was a primary school teacher, my biological father a lawyer, and my stepfather a mechanic.

I did not have a close relationship with my father, in fact, my stepfather was my best friend, teaching me to cook and to ride a bike. My father was not a weekend dad; rather he was a sporadic presence dropping in every so often. My mother on the other hand was a university student at the time of my birth and during my early formative years before she eventually qualified as a teacher.

Throughout my childhood she was always surrounded by paperwork including during the school holidays. Looking back, her inability to give me quality time and undivided attention was the reason that I vowed to never become a teacher. In my opinion she was too busy with thirty other people's children that she had no time for her own.

This may come as a surprise to many who now know me, but I was incredibly quiet as a child and was 'antisocial' to a point because I would sit and read books at birthday parties. My mum created a foundation focused on education and learning just as the Bible encourages, *"Train up a child in the way he should go: and when he is old, he will not depart from it."*[66] As an adult I still retained my love of reading however the

---

[66] Proverbs 22:6

'antisocialism' I once had, had well and truly gone with me going to the other extreme of talking too much.

So, what is my currency?

One word, time! Anyone who would give me quality time would fast became my best friend, as my late friend Minerva Stevens would have attested to. Despite the thirty-year age gap we were very close, and she was my rock. No matter where I was in the world she would telephone me, albeit she sometimes fell asleep on the phone due to the length of the call. When she died there was a huge void in my life that was never replaced. However, since her passing I had been blessed to meet occasional 'substitutes.'

The problem with some of those substitutes was that their intention hadn't always been pure, and typically they would come in the form of lewd men, and not just the single ones. As I would readily admit I talk a lot, but that does not mean to say that I told all of my personal business, on the contrary I took after my mother in being very secretive.

As I would often say, "I talk a lot, to disguise what I am hiding underneath." Many of my friends had no idea that I was the victim of sexual abuse because I never felt the need to tell them. Truth be told, a lot of my 'friends' didn't actually care or would be insensitive in telling me to move on because it had happened so long ago.

Consequently, time would become my vulnerability, in addition to affirmative words. Aside from my dislike of people talking about my physical attributes I thrive off words of encouragement.

I would occasionally make the joke that if a guy listened attentively to my problems, encouraged me and prayed with me I would marry him. That would not be completely far from the truth because the guy I fell in love with ticked off all of those boxes. There were of course many others, but they lacked in many areas, the biggest of which was their inability to respect and adhere to my boundaries in dating. I say this to say that despite time being my greatest vulnerability, due to my strong Christian morals and values, no matter how much time a guy would mete out to me I would not sleep with him or smuggle drugs or weapons. This is not to suggest that every Christian has that same willpower and strength to say no to such requests.

On the contrary, there have been promiscuous Christians, prostituted Christians and exploited Christians. Belonging to a particular faith is not necessarily a saving grace when the person has a weakness and that weakness is discovered and exploited by unscrupulous individuals.

As I would explain to my audience, any person could be trafficked, and not just for commercial sex. The solution to evading exploitation is to know your currency and when it has been identified by others. So, what are some of the various currencies that we could have?

- Time
  - o Listening ear
  - o Undivided attention

- Love
  - o Acceptance
- Affection
- Attention
  - o Feeling valued/important
- Money
  - o Materialistic items
- Sex

Now, this is not an extensive list, but what is most important to note is that our currency could sometimes change and include things like assistance; help; advice; support; directions.

A personal example of my change in currency concerned my travel lifestyle. As a volunteer I would frequently accept the kindness of strangers offering food, transport, accommodation, and even clothing. On one of my overseas trips I became acquainted with a pastor with the intention of obtaining speaking engagements. When we met I was incredibly vulnerable because of my current housing and financial situation.

I had absolutely no money, insufficient food and no freedom, therefore our first interaction was a huge relief for me as though I had just been let out of prison. The pastor garnered sufficient information which gave him a better understanding of what I was going through, which he wanted to take advantage of.

In this instance my currency was assistance and support to obtain speaking engagements. At face value that may seem farfetched, but when considered in the light of my rather dire circumstances, the pastor's ability or inability to create speaking opportunities for me could have made him my knight in shining armor. Unfortunately for me he failed to deliver despite having the means and connections to do so.

His intentions were never pure, and I did not think he was ever really sincere about helping me. On the contrary, considering that he was a married man, albeit his wife was overseas, I was under the impression that her absence somehow gave him the authority to prey on single females such as myself. His behavior was wholly inappropriate from inviting me round to his place for a home cooked meal; making reference to me sleeping at his house; and questioning me about my love life (albeit a nonexistent one) which was a topic that should never have been up for discussion.

Last but by no means least, the last time we were together he kept touching my knee and even touched my face under the guise that I was crying which was ridiculous because I would not need someone to tell me something that I could clearly work out for myself.

At the time, as old as I was, I felt as though I was being groomed. The pastor would never have succeeded in engaging me in an extra-marital relationship, but I believed he would have certainly continued trying.

In an instance, such as the one I described above, ignorant people would ask, "Why didn't you scream or hit him, or tell him to stop?" What such people failed to understand was that the pastor's behavior was very subtle, and in my opinion far from harmless. Some may disagree with me; in fact, I had a friend who tried to consider things from the perspective that the pastor's actions were innocent. Although I was not in his head, I wholly disagreed because I was convinced that if his wife had been in our company she would not have approved of his actions.

This was one of the greatest challenges I felt that victims sometimes had, the inability to fight back, even more so when the behavior was so unsuspecting. In other words, it could be so gradual that one day you would wake up after having engaged in unwanted sexual activity.

This is not to say that all men are predators, far from it. Males and females could become predators to unsuspecting individuals. The key is to be one step ahead and therefore avoid being ensnared.

Let's consider girls who had been abandoned by their biological parents and moved from one foster family to another. Without having been through that it would be difficult for us to understand the feelings of rejection that child was going through, their desire to belong and be loved. This desire would become the currency that a pimp or trafficker would use to get that girl to become putty in his or her hand.

In some instances, the pimp would begin by befriending the girl, getting her to open up, especially about her family life. This could go on for weeks with the pimp merely providing a listening ear. On occasion the pimp may make drugs and alcohol available to the girl, but with no pressure for her to engage. Eventually over time the girls guard would go down and her loyalty towards the pimp would go up. It was usually at this point that the pimp would begin a sexual relationship with the girl, which would lead on to demands for her to have sex with his 'friends.' At this point the girl would usually be plied with drugs and alcohol sometimes developing a substance dependency which would enable the pimp to keep her firmly under his or her control.

I began this chapter by emphasizing that every one of us has a need, from the youngest to the oldest. I do not believe that any one of us is too young to identify our currency; on the contrary I believe that it is a necessity. As the saying goes, the ability to change starts with accepting that you have a problem. Similarly, by knowing your currency you can make healthier relationship choices, rather than destructive ones.

So, the question I want to leave with you, "What is your currency?"

Signs and Symptoms of Childhood Sexual Abuse

♦

Signs and symptoms of childhood sexual abuse differ depending on a number of factors. This is not an exhaustive list, but aims to provide a basic guide to help you identify if there is a victim or survivor in your world.

The sad reality is that we are frequently surrounded by victims and survivors of sexual abuse, but are completely oblivious. Sometimes this is because we cannot even contemplate this as a possibility because in doing so we would apportion blame upon ourselves for not spotting the signs earlier or for intervening.

In my own personal story, I exhibited many of the signs and identifiers on the list below while also having a great interest in books particularly those written about child abuse. My tremendous fascination with programs on crime did not raise any eyebrows or any of the other behaviors I exhibited.

I believe that I have Stockholm syndrome which has not completely left my system. The best way to describe this in simple terms would be that you love your abuser either platonically or romantically. My stepfather was my best friend; therefore, my feelings of affection were

100% platonic. I never had any other feelings towards him besides that of a friend or stepfather.

I was groomed, which was something I was not aware of until about a few years ago when I attended a women's' breakfast at church and a young lady shared her story. Our stories were completely different; hers involved meeting older guys after school and engaging in illicit sex, while mine was about being violated in my sleep. That day was when I finally got the revelation that I was groomed; something I had been in denial about for many years because I had separated the abuse from the special privileges I'd been receiving.

Grooming can be summed up with one word: preparation, preparation for work, preparation for school, or preparation for sex. Grooming in the context of abuse or exploitation would be when someone does your hair, nails, makeup, takes you out for food; buys you Jordan's; takes you to the movies with the intention of exploiting you sexually. Grooming does not have to be sexual, but may be tangible or intangible and could even include giving time, love and affection.

To the outside observer I was very close to my stepfather, which they saw nothing wrong with. In fact, there were many people who were dumbfounded by my allegations because they had met and spoken with him in the past. I find that is often the problem. The pedophile lives behind a mask, showing different faces to different people, therefore when their crimes are eventually uncovered people are astonished, the revelation is completely unexpected.

My aim has been to get people to wake up and accept the realization that you cannot trust anybody. I do not want us to walk around as a paranoid set of people but instead to use wisdom, not make rash decisions or let our guard down.

We are in a society where anything goes including as I mentioned in the previous chapter a mother and daughter engaging in a consensual sexual relationship. Considering the things I'd read and heard about, nothing really surprises me, but I found that particular article sick and depraved. The result, when a mother starts engaging in sex with her 'consenting' adult daughter is how is any child safe? After all, if mother's are having sex with their children, what would stop teachers and students, doctors and patients etc.?

Abuse has always been rampant, and things will only get worse. There is therefore a need now more than ever before to understand the signs and symptoms of abuse so that a child could be whipped out of a dangerous situation as soon as it started. Having been a victim of childhood sexual abuse and met and spoken with dozens of survivors both male and female, I can say with a great deal of authority that these identifiers are indeed accurate many of which remain present in adulthood.

Cultural, environmental and familial upbringing has a lot to do with how we will develop as adults. There are many adults walking among us today who are fully functional, even successful at what they do, maybe even the life and soul of the party, with a spouse and children but there is something different about them, you just can't quite put your finger on it.

On occasion when I would go through this list of identifiers with my audience, someone would come up to me at the end of my presentation and share that a student popped into their head almost immediately. As soon as I heard that it led me to believe that it was highly likely that, that child had indeed been abused; which further emphasizes the importance of these lists.

Behavioral Indicators in Younger Children:

- "Mimics adult-like sexual behaviors" with toy or stuffed animals
- Resists removing clothes at appropriate times (bath, bed, toileting, diapering)
- Has new words for private body parts
- Asks other children to behave sexually or play sexual games"[67]
- Overeating or under-eating
- Compulsive behaviors
- Wetting the bed
- Sucking the thumb
- Regressive behavior
- Nightmares
- Unable to concentrate

---

[67] Stop It Now!, "Tip Sheet: Warning Signs of Possible Sexual Abuse In A Child's Behaviors, Accessed August 30, 2018. https://www.stopitnow.org/ ohc-content/ tip-sheet-7

■ Poor performance at school/can't concentrate[68]

Behavioral Indicators in Older Children:

■ Outbursts of anger

■ Depression

■ Withdrawal

■ Excessive bathing

■ Poor hygiene

■ PTSD

■ Overly compliant

■ Inability to make and sustain friendships

■ Runs away

■ School problems

■ Refuses to participate in school or social activities

■ Afraid of being home alone

■ Afraid of showers or washrooms

■ Insomnia

■ Compulsive behavior

■ Uncomfortable getting undressed in front of others

■ Promiscuity

■ Changes in eating habit

■ Excessively on the computer

■ Fear of going outside

■ Fearful of males or females

---

[68] Parents Protect!, "Warning Signs In Children And Adults", Accessed August 25, 2018. https://www.parentsprotect.co.uk/warning-signs-in-children- and-adults.htm.

- Insecure
- Low self-esteem
- Unusually secretive
- Very self-conscious about their body
- Suicidal tendencies
- Destructive behavior
- Cries without provocation
- Engages in prostitution
- Obtains new money, clothing or gifts
- Unintended pregnancy
- HIV/AIDS, STDs
- Alcohol or drug abuse
- Anxiety
- Uncomfortable with physical contact e.g. platonic hugs
- Lack of trust of others
- Hypertension[69]

If you identify a number of these signs in a child it is highly likely that the child has been abused or is currently being abused. It is therefore your responsibility to ensure that the necessary intervention takes place; the steps to follow will be discussed in the next chapter.

---

[69] *Ibid*

Disclosure of Sexual Abuse

♦

From my own personal experience of being sexually abused as a child, my desire was to educate people on how not to make the same mistakes that my mother and family made, which unlike many survivors was not a matter of being disbelieved but their mishandling of the situation.

The sad reality is that most parents educate their children that nobody should touch their body parts, and maybe even ask the child if they have been abused. This would usually take place during a conversation about good touches and bad touches, or good secrets and bad secrets.

The former would typically take place when the child was being washed or dressed, and would include pointingout and naming parts of their body. This is an important conversation that parents must have, but in my opinion, it is an inadequate safeguard especially when a child is groomed.

Similarly, I also have fault with teaching children the terms good secrets/bad secrets. First, the most obvious issue is that a child's immediate response to the question, "Can you keep a secret?" would be, "No," during childhood, and then "It depends" during adulthood.

Instead children should be taught to respond, "Yes" to, "Can you keep a secret?" but informed that the yes was only to hear the secret, not to be shown anything, and not to do anything. The best way to explain this is to teach your child to respond something like this, "Yes I will listen to you, and I will keep what you have told me a secret. But, I will not look at something that is secret, and I will not do something that is secret."

By responding in this way, you are educating your child on an appropriate response to what would often be a cry for help, whilst also safeguarding them from seeing or doing something that might constitute a 'secret.'

This may not be enough however, because some pedophiles would abuse a child and tell them, "This is our little secret." In such an instance, the child should 'agree' to keep the secret, but immediately reveal what happened when they are alone with their parents.

This sounds very straightforward in theory, however sometimes the child is threatened that they or their family will be arrested or killed if a disclosure of abuse is made. This fear usually succeeds in silencing the child into adulthood. However, truth be told this is often an empty threat as the average pedophile is a perverted coward and not a murderer.

Bearing this in mind, children should be told something similar to the following:

Disclosure of Sexual Abuse

"Sometimes a man, woman, boy, or girl may show you pictures or videos of naked people, or people having sex. They may take their clothes off, or make you take your clothes off. They may ask you to touch their private parts, or they may touch your private parts with the use of their hand or an object. They may have sex with you, or make you have sex with another boy or girl, or a man or woman while they watch. They may take photos or videos of you."

"If this happens to you, that man, woman, boy, or girl may tell you that it is your little secret. They may also tell you that if you tell mummy or daddy your secret that the police will arrest you or us and we will all be killed. If they say that or anything similar, then tell them that you will keep it a secret."

"Then as soon as you come home, wait until mummy and daddy are alone and tell us everything that happened. We will not be angry with you, we will be very happy that you told us. No matter what someone does to you or makes you do against your will, the police will not arrest you or arrest us. The police are here to protect us to make sure that no one will ever do that to you again, and they will keep us all safe so that no one can kill us. The police have safe houses where we can stay, and that nobody can find us. By you telling us the truth about what happened, mummy and daddy can protect you."

Once again, this isn't a verbatim script but an example of the kind of things that you could say, including with the use of names or titles such as aunty or uncle, since abuse was usually perpetrated by somebody that you knew.

The problem with the title aunty and uncle is its frequent use by children to address anyone who is older than them, including those of no relation. This is common practice in African and Caribbean circles as a sign of respect. The challenge with this is that it confuses small children who would see 'uncle' and 'aunty' kissing, since they are a married couple. Second, it creates over familiarity with strangers as typically biological aunts and uncles would exchange hugs and kisses with their nieces and nephews.

When everyone is addressed as uncle and aunty, where would the line be drawn to identify acceptable and unacceptable behavior? Instead, terms like sir, madam, Mr., or Mrs. should be deemed more acceptable.

You always need to be one step ahead of the pedophile by equipping your child to respond appropriately in a harmful situation, but also empowering them to make an immediate disclosure to you irrespective of the person's identity. You need to instill confidence in your child that no one is going to kill you or them because the police would protect you.

This conversation does not guarantee that your child would disclose that they have been abused particularly if they are groomed which also silences victims by distorting their perception of right and wrong.

I was groomed, which is something that I failed to accept because I had separated the abuse from the grooming, in fact I still do. Although I acknowledge being groomed, I still hold the belief that it was indirectly related to the sexual abuse. In the day time my stepfather gave me candy, let me stay up late and gave me alco-pops, whilst during the night he would abuse me as I slept.

As a child I hated my mother who was incredibly strict, my stepfather took advantage of this by becoming my best friend and giving me special privileges. My family disliked how close we were since my stepfather was not my peer, but they never once sat down and asked me about our relationship. They failed me in this aspect, plus their inability to respond appropriately when I asked them repeatedly, "Can you keep a secret?"

Now assuming that you answer, "Yes" or affirmative to that question and a child discloses their experience of being sexually abused, these are the next steps you would take:

1. Believe the child.

As controversial as this first step may seem it is of high importance despite how unbelievable the allegation may be.

Never brush off an allegation of sexual abuse if it did not involve physical sexual contact between the accused and the victim. This could very well be the case in many households when a child initially discloses an inappropriate sexual experience which is minimized or ignored as not being serious. When preventative action isn't taken it enables the accused to perpetrate the abuse again and escalate their sexual violation.

This is something I personally experienced during a vacation in Florida. I had returned to our apartment for some reason and was stood outside by the floor to ceiling window trying to get my stepfather's attention. He had been taking a shower at the time, so I patiently waited peering through a small gap in the curtains. My stepfather never let me inside, but instead stood completely naked in front of the mirror. Due to the position of the mirror I could see the front of his body in full profile.

When I rejoined my mother at the swimming pool and told her what had happened she defended my stepfather saying that he had not seen me. At that time without having prior knowledge of the years of sexual abuse I'd previously endured; her response could be deemed reasonable in the circumstances. However, when considered in the light of his future actions I would say that he used that as an opportunity to groom me.

Disappointingly my mum never addressed this incident with my stepfather. However, if she had indeed questioned him I feel certain that he would have denied seeing me and nothing further would have been thought about the incident.

My stepfather, as with other pedophiles, displayed inappropriate behavior that was merely shrugged off. This happens far too often resulting in re-victimization because the child is never truly heard. Phrases about being a voice to the voiceless are frequently thrown around but does society really know what that means?

I've found that quite often we would join rallies and marches to speak out on what was right, but when all had been said and done the voice that wasn't truly being heard was usually right at home. Bearing this in mind you'd become responsible for taking the child's story at face value, and believing they are telling the truth. In fact, you should feel honored that they had the confidence to share with you something so intimate and personal, especially as disclosing abuse takes a lot of courage and is probably one of the most difficult things that child had to do.

Consider the possibility that the accused had warned the child that no one would believe them. In such an instance your expression or words of disbelief would adversely affect them further solidifying the lies of the accused and out of fear could cause the child to recant their allegation. You would therefore need to separate yourself from the allegations and make yourself an outside observer. Your natural reaction would presumably be shock, even more so if you know the accused and could never imagine their capacity to enact such perverse behavior on a child.

The sad reality is that the vast majority of pedophiles are often hidden in plain sight, working respectable jobs, known as a pillar of the community, a devoted member of a religious faith and even sometimes married with children of their own.

The way that I look at it, is that people are people, and all capable of enacting crimes against another, therefore we should suspect everyone. Please understand, I am not advocating paranoia, my point is simply that we need to stop taking people at face value and realize that there is so much more beyond the surface that we do not see.

In the instance of a disclosure of sexual abuse, my advice would be to consider the accused 'guilty' unless proven innocent and irrespective of the minor fact that children sometimes lie, on that occasion your obligation would be to wholeheartedly believe the child.

2. Remain calm.

Depending upon the details of the disclosure and the identity of the accused you may be shocked to the point of an outburst of anger or rage. The problem with your reaction is that the victim could interpret that anger as being directed at them which they could have been forewarned of by the abuser.

In such an instance the predictability of your behavior as possibly explained to the child by the accused could lead that child to believe any other lies they'd been told to ensure they retained secrecy about the abuse.

They may then recant their earlier disclosure or even blame themselves for your reaction. That guilt coupled with shame could leave that child feeling responsible for being abused. They may not have shared with you the true extent of their experience and would be less likely to do so if they believe you are unable to handle the details.

This is not necessarily a bad thing because the less informed you are the better, however if you do display anger whether verbally or non-verbally you would need to explain to the child that you are not angry at them but are angry about what happened. Let them know how brave they have been in opening up to you but that you are simply feeling very hurt and upset and they are in no way to blame for that.

3. Ensure you are in a safe and private place to talk.

Due to the sensitive nature of the disclosure it is important that you are in a safe and private place away from any prying ears. It is paramount that you protect the child's testimony by not interviewing them and ensuring their disclosure remains confidential by speaking in a secure environment.

The aim is to prevent outsiders from listening in which could lead to rumors or the accused becoming informed, hiding or destroying evidence, or even silencing the child.

4. Reassure the child that there are other victims and survivors just like them.

Depending upon the nature and duration of the abuse, and the gender and identity of the perpetrator the child may believe that they have some abnormality and are the only one to have endured this experience.

The shame and secrecy that surrounds abuse make it particularly difficult for boys to disclose. They may feel a lot of guilt and blame, that they are responsible for their experience and have questions and doubts about their sexuality.

Depending upon the culture, sex may never be a topic of conversation leaving the child feeling isolated and even abnormal. Let them know that they are not the first child to have had this experience, possibly share your own experience if you were a victim and are comfortable doing so. Share success stories of survivors who were also abused but have not allowed their experience to destroy their lives, instead becoming productive and positive members of society.

5. Be transparent about what you can and cannot do.

You do not have the capacity to be the child's superhero and your scope of assistance can only go so far depending upon your relationship to them. Don't make promises no matter how sincere they may be. Let the child know that you will do everything in your power to help protect them and that there is an open line of communication for them to talk to you.

No matter how well-meaning you may be, avoid making any promises because if for some reason those promises are not fulfilled the child will no longer trust you.

6. Keep your opinions of the perpetrator to yourself.

Regardless of the perpetrator's identity do not vocalize any negative opinions about them or their behavior. It is unhelpful, even more so if they had a close or familial relationship with the child.

As difficult as it may be to get your head around, the child may still love or have feelings of affection towards the abuser. Those feelings would be particularly confused because the child did not like being abused but loved the 'other side' of the accused. Abusers often have many faces and if you know the accused personally and would never have suspected them then it's even more understandable that the child had affection towards them, especially if they were groomed.

7. Report the disclosure to the appropriate authorities.

Once you've learnt of a situation of abuse depending on whether or not you are a mandatory reporter you would have either a legal or moral obligation to inform the authorities immediately. Whether the country's protective system is effective or not is not a matter for consideration as your obligation is to take all necessary steps to protect the child.

Before involving the authorities however, it is paramount that you inform the child of the next steps that you are going to take and your reason for doing so. You would want to prevent them from feeling betrayed, and as best as you could alleviate the possibility of the child developing trust issues.

You would need to reassure the child that what had happened to them was wrong, they are not in trouble, but that the authorities have a duty to protect him/ her hence the reason you need their involvement. For example, you could say:

"What you shared with me is a crime; nobody should be touching your body or doing those things to you. You are not to blame, but I have a duty to protect you the best way that I can. Earlier on I told you that I can keep a secret, but I did not promise you that I would keep your secret. I don't want you to think that I lied, I did not lie. I have kept your secret for the last twenty minutes but now I am going to have to break your trust and call the police. I am doing this because it's my responsibility to ensure that you are safe and although I cannot protect you, I need to allow the authorities to help you where I can't. I want you to know that you can trust me therefore I will never go and do something without telling you first. I don't know how the police will help, but I have confidence that they will do what they believe is the best thing for you right now."

This is not a script for communicating your next steps to the child. The above is just to give you a general idea of the things you could say. Once the authorities have been informed you would then update the child as to what the authorities would do e.g. take a statement, have a video interview etc.

At no point should you alert the perpetrator, friends or family. Use complete discretion and retain confidentiality at all times.

8. Inform the child what will happen.

After speaking with the authorities you would be better informed of their next steps, which you must relay to the child.

Don't ever disregard the fact that the accused may have lied to the child about what would happen if they made a disclosure. It could have included things such as no one would believe them; the child would be arrested; their family would be incarcerated; they would be taken away to a children's home etc.

Bearing this in mind you would need to alleviate any possible fears the child may have by keeping them informed of the next steps, as well as the name and occupation of the appropriate people involved.

9. Let the authorities do their job, don't launch your own investigation.

During the child's disclosure you must not interrupt them but instead allow them to speak freely. Take contemporaneous notes and avoid asking questions unless you need clarity as to whether the disclosure involves abuse. Refrain from asking investigative questions which would prove harmful to the child's future court case. Leave all the details to the police.

10. Get support for yourself.

Hearing about the child's experience may deeply affect you, especially if you know the person or have also been a victim of abuse. You would need to keep the child's allegation confidential, but may need to talk with someone about what you heard. Seek help and assistance from a professional such as counselor so you could relieve yourself of everything you'd been feeling.

Why?

T he why question is not only necessary in relation to abuse but should always be asked mentally, particularly when to do so verbally would be deemed inappropriate.

My desire whenever I presented on human trafficking was never to leave behind an audience of likeminded robots. On the contrary, I wanted people to become more open minded, less judgmental, more community conscious and not just fixated on their own family but genuinely caring about the needs of others, instead of not caring about an issue until it landed on their doorstep.

At the end of the day whether we agree with this or not, sin has entered the world, and we have the free will to live, act and think as we please. Sadly, whenever an innocent life is taken or destroyed we get angry at God and ask, "Why?" Often the response we get back is silence.

I do not know or understand why there are newborn babies subjected to sexual abuse violations, torture, rape or murder for the pleasure of another human being. But I believe the more significant why question here should be, "Why is one human being sexually gratified by viewing or inflicting such atrocities against a defenseless life?" There are a number of reasons which include exposure to pornography, the result of childhood sexual abuse, a mental imbalance, etc. The list is indeed endless.

I believe that if we heard Peter Scully had been subjected to abuse his entire childhood we would think one of two things:

1. That he was programmed that way, or

2. Since he was a victim he should have known that what he experienced was wrong and not reenact those very same things on someone else.

I am not a psychologist nor am I versed in the study of the mind, but I do know that it really isn't that simple. The brain is very complex and is something that continues to be studied and analyzed to better understand why some individuals commit truly heinous crimes.

In the case of Peter Scully and one of his Filipino girlfriends Liezyl Margallo who was twenty-three at the time of her arrest, she had been working as a sex tour guide in Malapascua Island.[70] Liezyl had been prostituted as a child. Now, this does not in any way justify the sick sexual acts she performed upon Scully's

---

[70] M. G. Martin, "Fears that child abuser Scully is continuing vile video trade from behind bars", *PLN Philippines Lifestyle News*, January 30, 2017. https:// philippineslifestyle.com/fears-that-child-abuser-scully-is-continuing-vile- video-trade-from-behind-bars/

victims, but it can somewhat help to explain who she is and why she did what she did.

Sadly, the world is made up of judgmental people who are ignorant about a particular subject matter but still form a strong opinion. This is particularly evident when a young girl becomes pregnant outside of marriage. Irrespective of the fact that she did not get pregnant alone, she would often receive a lot of negativity and criticism by peers and adults alike.

In my opinion, whenever an underage girl is pregnant, we need to mentally ask ourselves the question, "Who is the father?" Now I must point out that I said mentally, as I am not advocating questioning the girl. Furthermore, unless you are 100% certain of the identity of the father and the manner of conception, what right do you have to cast judgment because the pregnancy may have been the result of incest or rape.

If a girl or boy is promiscuous, instead of judging that behavior, ask yourself mentally, "Why?" What about if you observe a small child pulling down their pants or skirt? Don't just shrug it off, or laugh and say, "They are just being children." When I was a child I could never have done that. I was taught by my mum how to dress and undress in private, therefore whenever I saw a small child pulling down their pants or skirt and laughing I would ask myself, "Who else are they entertaining?"

How about uncovering an instance of abuse, where does the "Why?" question fit in?

181

Let me give you two examples of the "Why?"

1. I asked my friend, "Why did you open your Christmas present before Christmas day?" She replied, "How did you know that?" I said, "I didn't, you just told me."

2. I asked my mum, "Why didn't you tell me that grandma called?" She replied, "Grandma didn't call."

Thanks to popular belief, lawyers are often referred to as professional liars, dishonest, deceitful etc. As a new lawyer without any prior cross examination skills or training I determined that if I wanted an honest response I had to feign knowledge of the answer, hence my questions would always start with why.

Let's look at the "Why?" in relation to sexual abuse, you may ask, "Why did you let uncle lift up your skirt?" Or maybe, "Why did you let aunty touch your private parts?"

I can't give you a script because it all depends on the circumstances, but my advice has always been to start your question with "Why?"

Is this foolproof? Of course not, remember this is a book and you will not be the only person reading it. This is merely a guideline, so for you to be convincing you would have to make the question your own just always start with the word "Why?"

Stories of Childhood
Sexual Abuse

America

■ A 7-year-old girl came to school and said, "Daddy is   eating my cookie."

The girl was referring to her genitals but because the word 'cookie' was used it wasn't uncovered until much later that she had been describing sexual abuse.

■ A young boy was sexually abused in the restroom by a peer and again at nursery by a member of staff during the prayer meeting.

He became very angry as a young boy because of the abuse he was subjected to and turned his back on Christianity until many years later when he became a pastor.

England

■ A woman wanted her boyfriend to be sexually satisfied so she asked him what he would like. He requested photographs and she in turn took photos of herself sexually abusing her 6-month-old baby girl.

If that mother was never caught and arrested and that child was subjected to abuse her entire life, what would happen when she went on to have her own 6-month-old baby girl? She would likely do the exact same thing. However, notably, this is not always the case. Joyce Meyers and Oprah Winfrey were both victims of childhood sexual abuse and as far as we know they are most certainly not pedophiles.

Trinidad and Tobago

■ A girl was sexually abused around the age of ten, when she was about 12-years-old a boy of similar age came up to her and said, "Touch my genitals," so she did.

For the average judgmental adult, they would assume that this girl was promiscuous but in fact she was not. It could almost be considered a learned behavior which many of us would not understand.

■ A boy was sexually abused by his female nanny. When he entered high school he would get to school early and have sex in the back of the classroom.

When I heard this story it made me really angry. I found the boy's actions completely disrespectful since he could very easily have gone outside and had sex in the field.

There is a scripture in the Bible that says, *"Do not arouse or awaken love until it so desires."*[71] In this boy's case, he was sexually abused at a young age which made him aware of his sexuality before the right time, which I believe is during marriage.

---

[71] *Supra* 42

- A girl was sexually abused by a male family member.

  When she entered a sexual relationship in her late twenties, she would ask her male partner to be violent towards her during sex because without him realizing she wanted to enact what she had experienced at the hands of her relative.

- A girl was sexually abused by many of her male relatives.

  She was often dressed in black from head to toe with a sweater or other baggy top that completely enveloped her torso and arms down to her wrists. Her teacher and peers were concerned because of how withdrawn she seemed and had genuine fears that she was cutting her wrists.

- A boy was sexually abused as a young child by a female adult.

  As a man he still struggled with the effects of what had been done to him and it caused him great difficulty in his marriage.

- A girl was sexually abused by four out of five brothers.

  As a result of being abused repeatedly she held her one brother in high esteem since he hadn't victimized her, and she believed that she would become a lesbian.

- A girl was sexually abused by her teacher.

  She disclosed this to her father and the police were informed.

- A baby under a year old was sexually abused by her 17-year-old brother.

  This was only uncovered during the medical examination when the baby died as a result of her injuries.

- A boy came to school and was upset because his mum was pregnant. The teacher asked him why he wasn't excited about the new arrival. He shared that he was upset because he didn't know if the baby was his or his brothers.

  When I heard this story, I was floored despite knowing that biological mothers sometimes sexually abuse their children.

- A number of boys engaged in sexual activity with goats in Tobago.

  People usually found this really hilarious, but it really wasn't, I felt sorry for the goats because as a vegan I believe that 'Goat Lives Matter.'

  The question we need to ask ourselves is where is this behavior coming from? Most young people engage in sexual activity with another human being not an animal. However, with the legalization of bestiality in Canada and animal brothels in Europe it should really not come as a surprise that people of all ages are developing a sexual interest towards animals.

My Story

♦

I do not really remember how it all started but our holiday in Spain is my first recollection of being abused.

Whenever I addressed my audience I would make the statement that, "100% guaranteed one of you in this audience, male or female has indeed been the unfortunate victim of childhood sexual abuse and you know who you are. I can guarantee that every time I'm in a room with at least three females."

On one occasion after making that statement a woman seated in the audience amongst the seven other participants shook her head profusely. That really bothered me and so as direct as I am I said, "You don't need to shake your head. For all you know the victim is sitting right beside you, may even be a male and you've just made them feel uncomfortable."

My question is, "What did shaking one's head profusely prove? Is being a victim of abuse a terrible thing; is that individual stigmatized?"

At the end of the day none of us can truly guarantee that we have not been sexually abused because our recollection only goes back so far. In fact, I know of two girls who were both sexually abused as children but neither of them knew it. One of the survivors had flashbacks; the other was in a children's home where she had been placed following sexual abuse at the hands of a family member between the ages of one to six months old. How many of us remember what took place between the ages of one to six months? I confidently assume none of us.

There is so much shame that surrounds being abused although we were innocent victims. That shame and guilt often cripples us, affecting the decisions we make, the relationships we build and the perception and image we have of ourselves and others.

When I was four in an apartment in Spain my stepfather had been tickling me and his hand 'slipped.' Now, my mum has an issue with the way I phrased that experience, maybe I said it like that because my recollection of the incident is as a 4-year-old, so I used the age appropriate language that 'His hand slipped.'

As an adult I know that it did not slip but was an intentional act. Even while typing this I feel very uncomfortable with what I experienced despite it being 'just a slip.'

I had been taught as a young child that no one should touch my body parts. I remember those conversations as though it were yesterday. Unfortunately, those conversations did not help because I was groomed and subsequently abused over a 6-year period between the ages of four to ten.

Things always unfolded in the same way. The telephone would ring, and it would be my mum's friend with a reputation for talking too much. My stepfather would come upstairs, enter my bedroom, sexually abuse me, then leave and go into the bathroom, flush the toilet and then go back downstairs when the call had ended.

The specific details of what I went through serve no purpose as the average individual can simply use their imagination as to what I endured pre-BDSM days; suffice to say I was a victim of both digital rape and attempted rape and subjected to other unwanted bodily invasions. My experience was horrible and painful, and I never once enjoyed or found pleasure in what was done to me. I did not want to be interfered with sexually and wanted it to stop. I was only a small child when I fell prey to the lusts of a sick individual who used the excuse that he too had been the victim of sexual abuse by an aunt.

My stepfather was an alcoholic which was the excuse my mum made for his deviant actions. In my mind intoxication had absolutely nothing to do with it. He had a sexual interest towards me as a child and the alcohol gave him the confidence to act out his desires. I say this because the last time I checked alcohol did not come with a disclaimer: Warning! Consuming this beverage may result in several unintended side effects, including causing the consumer to sexually abuse a child.

Being a victim of attempted rape, I cannot imagine how violated a child would feel being subjected to rape, whether or not they were a virgin prior to the incident. It is truly only the grace of God that hindered my stepfather from actual penetration despite how persistently he had tried. Even typing this gives me great discomfort as stories of child rape flash before my eyes.

There are many people who cannot stomach hearing about abuse which greatly frustrates me because I believe that the very least they could do for the victim is hear what had been endured so that they could experience just a smidgen of pain. Whenever I shared the story of Daisy's destruction (in reference to the pornographic video made by Peter Scully) some of my audience members would cry out in utter shock. It was the only 'shock' story that I used and it was one I believed was necessary to make the reality of abuse sink in.

Daisy went through the most horrific abuse the Philippines had ever seen; the information detailed in newspaper articles did nothing to depict the full extent of her ordeal and the sad reality is that there are children who have experienced even worse. Bearing that in mind the question or topic of a person's virginity is a very insensitive subject and I hold a firm belief that the virginity of a man or woman, boy or girl should never be a subject up for discussion regardless of whether you are the same gender of the person you are asking. Virginity is not the be all and end all because if it was there would be no hope for the newborn babies and toddlers who were subjected to rape.

I could have lost my virginity as a 4-year-old if I had not fought back time and time again, and such a revelation would certainly put a dampener on any conversation. Whenever people would ask me about my virginity I became enraged because it was nobody's business but mine and my future husband's! Not my friend, colleague, acquaintance, boyfriend or even fiancé. The specifics of my sex life should never have been the focus of break time conversation at work and the fact that I wear a purity ring does not give license for inquiries about my virginity. My response has simply been that a purity ring is not about the past but the present. A person could have a child and wear a purity ring thereafter because they had made a future decision to save sex for marriage.

My story of abuse is not the first of its kind and sadly would not be the last. When the police were eventually informed of my historic case of abuse they were not convinced that I had succeeded in fighting off my stepfather. It wasn't that they doubted the veracity of my story but rather that I may have repressed some of the memories. Disappointingly my case did not get to court and although I had tried to revive it this was to no avail. Justice was never served in the eyes of the law leaving me to pick up the pieces.

Talking to my mum about the abuse year's later she explained her mistaken belief that my stepfather had been using the computer or the toilet (because he had constipation). This made no sense to me because I could not understand why he would all of a sudden leave from watching T.V. to go on the computer because of the

191

minor distraction of a very much one-sided phone call? I am however convinced that my mum had absolutely no idea what was going on, after all he had a daughter of his own so why would she suspect him abusing someone else's daughter? When she eventually found out however, her response was neither accountable nor protective.

One of my biggest regrets was that I did not inform the police whilst the abuse was ongoing. During my childhood there was no 'C.S.I. T.V. series,' but maybe if there were I would have understood the significance of DNA and trace evidence. The day in question that really springs to mind was when I woke up to the sound of my stepfather snoring beside me in my bed.

I got up, went downstairs and attempted to get into the living room which was barricaded with the sofa. When I eventually squeezed inside, I woke my mum up and told her that my stepfather was in my bed. Her eyes which were bloodshot looked directly at me before she closed them and fell back to sleep. She has always adamantly denied this, a denial with very little weight since she can hardly remember what had happened a week ago. I have no motivation to lie and my recollection of that incident has always been very vivid particularly because I had a very uncomfortable night's sleep curled up on the bamboo chair in my mother's bedroom.

If I had indeed called the police the evidence would have been overwhelming, there would have been saliva in my ear and possible other trace evidence on my skin and clothing, and my stepfather would have been found in my bed. As the saying goes, 'knowledge is power.' My lack of knowledge was why I did nothing when I had the chance. Calling the police as a child was scary, while talking about sex and body parts was embarrassing and uncomfortable. The shame I felt was why I had kept my secret for all those years and having been a victim myself I understand the importance of breaking the silence which I am doing through writing this book.

Now please understand despite the experience that I went through my mum did her best; she did not use the words, "Cookie, pumpkin, or butterfly." She gave me the right information but made these wrong decisions:

1. She unknowingly married a pedophile.
2. She chastised me the first time I disclosed I was abused.
3. She did not protect me after the abuse ended and I made a full disclosure of what had happened.

1. She unknowingly married a pedophile.

My biological parents were never married, the specifics as to why are of no importance to this story. Suffice to say I never grew up with my father; he was absent my entire life only popping up every so often.

He and I are both lawyers' albeit of different jurisdictions, however my reason for choosing that career path had absolutely nothing to do with him. In fact, the reason it took me so long to become a lawyer was because he kept forcing me to study law and I was resistant.

I never looked up to him as any kind of role model despite his past achievements and accolades. It is disappointing to say that he never helped me, whether that was studying for my law degree, being interviewed for a position at the Legal Aid Society in New York; or acquiring work experience in a U.K. law firm.

Instead my dad is not a "Yes be yes, no be no"[72] person but has a habit of over-promising and rarely delivering. This is a fundamental difference between the two of us, but genes do not hide and there are many parts of my character and personality that resemble him identically. Sadly, I have not taken many of the positives from my father's gene pool and consequently instead of graduating with an A at university I got the equivalent of a B+ which was still a tremendous achievement.

I would definitely say that I was born to be a lawyer; I think like one and talk like one. I believe it is a gift from God but will also accept that maybe genes play a tiny part in it too even more so since I have yet to have my day in court.

When I was four my mum married husband number one, Anthony Charles Brown who we called Tony for short. I never referred to him as Dad because I had a father and that man was not him.

I liked him instantly! We became very close and he was my best friend. Unlike my mother who was a teacher he was a mechanic. He was a handy man, was very good

---

[72] *"But let your communication be, Yea, yea; Nay,nay"* Matthew 5:37 (KJV)

around the house and also a fantastic cook which won points in everybody's book because my mum's food was tasteless.

He would have been described as handsome and very personable. My use of the past tense is because he is deceased and hopefully in hell for what he did to me. He screwed up my life and although I am a survivor he stole my innocence, leaving me still suffering from the effects of his depraved actions. I believe that if it wasn't for what he had done to me I would be married with my orphanage in the Philippines and adopted children. I would not have been travelling around the world for free trying to find my healing. Despite that, I believe, *"That all things work together for good to them that love God"*[73] and *"You intended to harm me, but God intended it for good."*[74]

My stepfather smoked cigarettes and was an alcoholic. He also suffered with constipation and had bad breath. These were incredibly significant because they played a part in my abuse.

2. She chastised me the first time I disclosed I was abused.

When the abuse first began it started with tickling. I told my mum immediately and she spoke to my stepfather and me. He ran away that night but sadly returned which enabled the abuse to continue.

---

[73] Romans 8:28 (KJV)

[74] Genesis 50:20 (NIV)

Looking back, I believe that this is where my mum made a fundamental mistake. By her own admission when I told her what had transpired with my stepfather she told both me and him off. Her words to me were, "Don't let it happen again." Now as a 4-year-old, those words placed responsibility upon me the child. Instead she should have thanked me and encouraged me to tell her if it happened again. Consequently, from that day forward for the next six years I made no further disclosures to my mum.

3. She did not protect me after the abuse had ended and I made a full disclosure of what had happened.

I told my female cousins whilst the abuse was ongoing, and they wisely informed their mother. The rest of my family became privy to my disclosure and we were supposed to have a meeting with my stepfather. That meeting never happened.

After the abuse 'stopped,' between the ages of eleven and sixteen my stepfather and I were home alone as was often the case. I walked into his bedroom and he was lying fully clothed on the bed. He lifted up the waistband of his trousers and asked me to put my hand inside. Despite the previous years of abuse I was naïve, I looked down and saw his pubic hair, I said "No" and walked away. However, if things had been different I would have acquiesced and entered into a 'consensual' sexual relationship.

What's sadder still is when a male relative had asked me if I wanted a relationship with my stepfather? The abuse started when I was 4-years-old so that question was simply preposterous. I told my mum who did nothing using the excuse that she had not been present to hear it. In my mind, once again she was not protecting me.

A number of years later a female relative wrote me some very hateful e-mails stating that I was angry at my mum for divorcing my stepfather because I had wanted a relationship with him, she also called me promiscuous and said that I would contract HIV/AIDs. For someone who was a virgin that re-victimization hurt tremendously.

When I likened myself earlier to Joseph in the Bible people often fail to understand since they are not aware of the betrayal I have repeatedly experienced at the hands of my family. Rumors concerning my sex life as a child and young adult have been rampant and that's all they were rumors since I had no sex life. On the contrary if I had even half as active a sex life as they described I would not have been single for all those years.

Years earlier when I was sixteen, I broke my finger. The circumstances surrounding this injury were deemed farfetched by some people who were unwilling to believe my version of events. That day upon returning home from school I turned on the television as usual. Normally I would get undressed in front of the T.V. but on that occasion I decided not to. When my mum came home she said that I had been filmed watching T.V. when I should have been doing my homework. I had been caught in the act.

I cannot recall the specifics, but my stepfather told me that he had the video of me watching T.V. In my mind I was quietly thanking God that I had not gotten undressed in front of the T.V. (even though I would never have been completely naked at any point because the abuse had made me very uncomfortable with my body).

My stepfather asked if I wanted to watch it on the television screen or on the video camera. I opted for the video camera. I peered over his shoulder as he cued the video. The video was not of me, I proceeded to watch for a minute longer but to no avail. The video was a homemade pornographic video of my mother and stepfather.

I left the bedroom where we had been sitting on the futon. I tripped, fell against the door and fractured my finger. As far-fetched as this story may sound that is exactly what happened. When my dad came to the hospital the next day he asked me if my stepfather had broken my finger and if I had been sexually abused. I denied both allegations.

A few years earlier when the abuse had 'stopped' the disclosure came out from a friend. This was the second time these allegations had been raised but again nothing was done, instead my mum told me to put something in front of my bedroom door to protect myself.

It wasn't until a few months before my sixteenth birthday when my stepfather was finally kicked out; more than a decade after the sexual abuse had first begun.

Around that time I had become close with a male relative who had been grooming me for sex, while at the same time telling my mum stories of my alleged promiscuity with boys from the secondary school next door. In doing so when he would have eventually raped me, my mum would have believed that I had enticed this relative because of my supposed sexual deviance.

Accusation after accusation continued to surface, all of which were untrue. The sad reality is that the people who should have known me better believed all the rumors, why? I was a victim in the past, so it made complete sense to them that I would behave in that way. Once again I experienced re-victimization.

The sad thing about the male relative's accusations is that I only discovered them years later. Sadder still is when I asked my mum if she had believed him, she had said, "You would have been sick in the head if you did that." I askedher again what was clearly a closed question requiring either a yes or no response but her response remained unchanged. Now I am sure you can all agree that my mum would make a terrible witness in court because of her refusal to play ball and answer the question.

The Bible says, *"by their fruit you will know them."*[75] One of the most painful things is that people who met me for a number of hours, days or weeks could tell by my character that I do not have a sexually deviant bone

---

[75] *Supra* 19

in my body. In fact, I would often make fast friends because I am such an open book.

People often wondered why, (considering how devoted of a Christian I am) I have failed to *"Honor thy father and mother."*[76] Why I spend as minimal time in England as possible and why I do not like my family? That is exactly why. Is my behavior appropriate? Of course not, have I forgiven my mother? I do not know the answer to that question.

She has made mistakes and I have suffered the consequences. Does that make her a bad person? No it does not. I am an only child and the only thing I have ever required from her is time, something she is unwilling to give.

Generally speaking, people often do not understand the value of time. It is the reason many individuals have affairs, walk away from relationships and often why women date men ten or more years older than them because, "He listens to me."

We all have different love languages and having not read the book I am not versed on those five languages, but what I can say is that time is incredibly valuable so my encouragement to you is to give it in abundance to the people in your life. It is free and costs nothing, but is often one of the hardest things for people to give.

---

[76] Ephesians 6:2 (KJV)

Forgiveness is important, it does not validate the hurt or wrong a person has done to you, it is not your assent to their action or inaction, nor does it require reconciliation. Forgiveness is for you not the other person, therefore a lack of forgiveness is like eating rat poison and expecting the rat to die.

Have I forgiven my stepfather? I do not know the answer to that question. He was the only stepfather I've had because although my mum has remarried, her spouse is simply 'my mum's husband.' Despite the hurt and pain inflicted upon me by my stepfather I can only view him in a positive light. I am in no way in denial that he was a pedophile, but he was my best friend who taught me to ride a bike and how to cook. He is the reason I developed a passion for culinary arts thus despite the evil he bought into my world I am unwilling to deny that he added a measure of positivity in my life.

The average individual would find that statement difficult to grasp, but in my opinion I feel that it is a lot 'healthier' to focus on the positives in a person rather than the negatives. Being angry and bitter will never restore my innocence and all that was stolen. My experiences have shaped me into the person that I am, but am I thankful for my experience? Absolutely not! Am I angry about what happened? Of course! But will my anger change anything? The answer to that is "No!"

I can never turn back the clock nor can I change the past, instead I have chosen to make my life productive. I have taken the negatives that I endured and made them positive. I will never understand why I became a victim of sexual abuse or why I could not have had a healthy and whole start to life like many other children. How I wish my life was different, that therapy is not the prerequisite to marriage, that I could have enjoyed the blessing of friends for the long-term instead of for a season. I do not have those things, but the Bible is my constant reminder that by Jesus stripes I am healed.[77]

I believe that healing is available to all. I do not have the magic cure and really wish that such a thing existed. Even though it does not, this does not make healing any less of a reality to all of those who share similar stories of abuse. My past does not dictate my future; I am doing something positive and productive with my life. I am simply an ordinary person doing extraordinary things without support, without money and without a fully-fledged team behind me.

I do not endorse Joyce Meyers or Oprah Winfrey, but I cannot deny the 180-degree transformation of their lives which began with childhood sexual abuse. The world does not need another Meyers or Winfrey, but it does need more survivors to rise above their start in life and do something that will have a noteworthy impact on the lives of others and society as a whole. I believe that someone could be you!

---

[77] *"[w]ith his stripes we are healed"*. Isaiah 53:5 (KJV)

My Six Years
Volunteering Unpaid

♦

Over the last six years I have led a faith filled life travelling around the world without a day job or money in the bank. Since people would always ask me how I could afford such luxuries without an income this book would be incomplete if I omitted sharing at least part of my story, so here goes:

Since December 2012 I travelled between the U.S. and Canada, or the U.S. and Jamaica for visa runs every six months. Whilst in the States I volunteered without pay providing free legal advice as part of the Christian Legal Society and a number of other Nonprofits throughout the New York area.

At the same time I was also studying for the New York Bar exam which I finally passed on my third attempt. Living in America for two years was not easy because not only were my finances minimal at best, but it was a very expensive place to be.

My money never dried up but would always be replenished, quite often as a result of the generous gifts of friends that came with such frequency that even in the absence of a paid job I would be tithing[78] almost every Sunday.

One such occasion of financial provision was when I walked up to the church altar for prayer following an invitation to the congregation. The pastor told us to pray with the person beside us. Now on my left was a Chinese lady and on my right was an African American woman that I usually made small talk with. I did not want to pray with the lady I knew so decided to pray with the Chinese woman despite my initial concern that she did not speak English, she did.

I told her that my prayer request was for the provision of accommodation that very same day. She prayed for me and then after we said "Amen" we turned back to the stage and proceeded to sing the worship songs. Before we returned to our seats the lady turned to me and gave me a HSBC envelope saying, "God told me to give this to you." I took it, walked back to my seat, and upon opening it on the walk back to my hostel I found $200.00 inside. After setting aside my tithes, there was exactly enough money for five more nights' stay in the hostel.

Another time I had a bank balance of approximately $9.00. I had been sharing my plight with a friend who did not understand how I had been managing with very little finances. After church as we walked back to

---

[78] *"Bring the whole tithe into the storehouse.... 'Test me in this,' says the Lord Almighty, 'and see if I will not throw open the floodgates of heaven and pour out so much blessing that there will not be room enough to store it."* Malachi 3:10-11 (NIV)

her house she asked me to give her a number between one and ten. I had been thinking of the numbers two and seven possibly because my birthday fell on August 27th. In the end I said nine. My friend then went straight to the cash machine and gave me $900.00. I tithed 10%, ordered cheese-less pizza from Pizza Hut, paid my rent and made some other extraneous purchases. The money that remained was a lot less than the original $810.00 but was nonetheless the exact amount necessary for a 1-way flight ticket back to England.

A few months before my trip to India I had yet to raise sufficient funds for my intended five month stay. I had been talking to a friend one night and distinctly remember saying, "Although I have only $900.00, it's enough money for a place like India, all I need is a flight ticket."

Just days before this conversation, I had attended a Continuing Legal Education (CLE) training for new lawyers. It was another great networking opportunity, so I made the effort to introduce myself to a number of the presenters, one of whom specialized in criminal defense. He was wonderfully charismatic, and I could not wait to meet him. We had a brief chance to talk and it was exactly that, brief. I was disappointed by our initial interaction but sent along a customary follow-up e-mail as was my usual procedure. To my surprise he responded almost immediately, and we exchanged a number of emails where I shared about my upcoming trip to India.

I also wrote about my heart for serving others around the world so passionately that the attorney mistook me for a missionary. In fact, he told me that he was so touched by something I had written that he had read my e-mail twice.

That night when I went to bed I realized that I had learnt the important lesson of not being so quick to write somebody off on the basis of my first interaction with them.

The next morning, whilst on my train journey into Manhattan my phone notified me of an incoming email. It was from a different e-mail account, where spam and other non-important messages would be received. I opened my inbox only to be left wide mouthed and speechless! I had received a $1,200.00 donation from the attorney. I could not believe it, just the night before I had been saying to my friend that "All I needed was money for a flight ticket," and then a huge donation arrived the very next day, as though God and the attorney had been listening in to my conversation.

A few years later when I was living in D.C. and unable to pay my rent, a friend called me and shared how he and his wife wanted to bless me financially provided I was willing to accept their help. I of course replied yes, provided him with my bank details and he blessed me with $1,000.00.

Around that same time when I had first lost my volunteer position a fellow attorney friend gave me $500.00 to pay for my outstanding month's rent; it was completely unexpected but definitely needed and appreciated.

While in the Philippines I often travelled from country to country on monthly visa runs for flights costing anywhere between $20.00 - $50.00 round-trip. There was no magic to the cost of my tickets it was simply that the value of money was vastly different in Asia enabling the average Westerner to live like kings and queens.

On a flight between two Filipino islands I was seated by the window with a gentleman to my left. His features resembled that of a South Indian or Sri Lankan but the passport he was holding did not come from either country. I continued to 'discreetly' scrutinize the front cover of his passport in an attempt to establish his ethnicity but eventually gave up and asked him where he was from. He was Australian. I had not been expecting that response, but he did explain that his parents were indeed Sri Lankan.

We talked for the duration of the 1-hour flight with him sharing that he was a medical doctor that did short term medical missions around the world once or twice a year. I told him about the work I had been doing around the Philippines and my passion for serving others. We swapped contact information with the doctor promising to fly me to the president's hometown in Davao for a human trafficking presentation.

We stayed in touch with the odd WhatsApp message every so often and then about a week before I was due to leave the Philippines he sent me the good news that my human trafficking presentation had been confirmed, and that he had booked and paid for my hotel and flight tickets. I was over the moon, for the first time in my life I had met someone who made and kept an extraordinary promise.

As I sat in the airport ready to board my plane I was truly in awe. Never in my wildest dreams could I have envisioned receiving all expenses paid flights and accommodation by a fellow passenger, but that was my God, using the kindness of a complete stranger who made an investment albeit a loan, (that I would eventually repay once I attained gainful employment).

On my trip to Davao I had a lengthy layover in Manila. My arrival was on time at 9 a.m. but I was not due for departure until 3.30 p.m. Since church is important to me, I did a Google search for the nearest one. The one that I found had already begun, but there was another service beginning at 11.30 a.m. that I decided to attend.

I made my way across town arriving over an hour early. There was a coffee shop nearby so I grabbed a seat outside so I could comfortably eat my packet of dry crackers and drink my lukewarm bottle of water. I was hungry but simply could not afford to buy anything inside, so I merely sat and bade the time.

I noticed a black lady walking towards me, so I called out to stop her, we began talking but she seemed to be in a rush. When she told me her occupation I knew it would be a great connection for me to have so I tried to locate my business card since she did not have one of her own. I could not find it, but continued talking, mentioning in passing that I was going to church. She was actually going to church too and it happened to be the same one.

We walked inside together while I shared with her my last experience that had been complete hell. As the service was about to begin I said goodbye and located a seat closer to the front. The sermon that day was exactly what I needed to hear because it spoke directly to the situation I had just endured.

After the service as I was walking out I bumped into the lady from earlier, she had been waiting for me. She told me how God had really been speaking to her the last couple of days and that she had a spare room she was going to clean out and prepare for me if I needed it. I said "Yes, I would need a place that weekend." Before we separated she gave me a 'Pentecostal hand shake,' when I eventually opened my hand I was floored. The money she had given me was the equivalent of a fortnight's salary in the Philippines.

Before she left she told me it was to buy lunch. That money was more than enough for breakfast, lunch and dinner, vegan style. Not only did I have free flights and free accommodation, but now I also had free 'lunch.'

When I returned from my trip to Davao I took a cab to the lady's house. It was a palace. The downstairs lobby looked like a hotel and her apartment was beyond beautiful. I had no idea such luxury existed in the Philippines. The bedroom was beautiful with en-suite bathroom and the dining table was elegant. When I had initially accepted her offer of a place to stay I had no idea what lay before me, it was simply amazing.

In India I had a similar experience following a church service. That day having stuck around for the youth service, I found a seat close to the front as was customary. I was later joined by a young lady who shared that she'd just finished studying in upstate New York.

After the service I had been talking to some of the guys when the lady from earlier approached me and extended an invitation for lunch. We joined her brother in the car and drove to their home. As we got out of the car I asked her if the guy driving us was her dad to which she replied he was her driver.

As we walked towards the house I had no idea what to expect as everything seemed incredibly ordinary, that was until the front doors opened and we were met with metal detectors, huge dogs and body guards.

To my utter astonishment I had just arrived at the home of the Chief Minister of Meghalaya, Mukul Sangma, the equivalent of hanging out at the President's home. I had absolutely no idea that I was in the company of a high- profile family, all I knew was that I'd become acquainted with a beautiful oriental looking woman who'd been a student in New York.

The food we ate that night was some of the best I'd ever tasted in India and breakfast the next morning was like heaven on a plate. I moved in for what was the best four days of my entire trip. My new friend and her brother had bodyguards and a chauffeur, I actually felt like royalty even though the security detail were obviously not for me.

My Six Years Volunteering Unpaid

On more than one occasion I had the privilege of meeting Mukul Sangma and on my last night there in the early hours of the morning (before getting on a 27-hour train ride to Delhi) I baked him my infamous chocolate cake with fudge frosting whilst we discussed ways I could contribute to his country.

Looking back on that experience it was simply unbelievable and is a memory I treasure fondly, not to mention our day of sightseeing and zip lining across five picturesque mountains. Disappointingly, I never saw or heard from the minister's daughter again despite making multiple attempts at contacting her. Aside from me wanting to enlist her as my bridesmaid and soloist (at my future wedding in Manipur, North East India), she really loved the Lord and her relationship with Him was inspiring.

In Trinidad I had a radio interview during the Sunday lunch hour. I headed there after the church service where I had just been having a private conversation with God about my immediate need for free accommodation. This was my first time on that particular program therefore I had no idea that it would also be live streamed online.

That day, unlike my previous radio interviews the lines were ringing off the hook with caller after caller commending me for the work that I do and praising my obedience to God (despite it not being a Christian radio station). At one point, overwhelmed by so much affirmation I became distracted whilst another caller was on the line. It was a lady who had been saying, "In this day and age you can't trust people, it's not safe to have any and everybody in your home but my place is available." I looked up and saw the radio host was smiling, I replied, "I'm a bit confused, can you repeat that?" The lady again said that she was providing me a place to stay rent free. I exclaimed, "Praise the Lord, I'm moving in tonight."

I did not actually move in that night despite visiting the house and having no major issues with it. God had somewhere so much better for me at my friend's place. He too had heard me on the radio and only then discovered that I needed accommodation, he then kindly opened up his home and for the next week and a half I lived in another beautiful 'palace,' this time complete with swimming pool.

A few weeks later I moved into yet another 'palace' for five days with hosts who blessed me with food and designer clothes. On the day of my arrival the husband had told me that I was welcome to stay until my departure three weeks later, explaining that his home was designed with visitors and guests in mind.

Day five of my stay quickly arrived when I would be heading to Tobago. In my spirit God spoke to me very clearly, leaving me convinced that the invitation I'd originally received to stay until September 20th no longer existed. God also revealed to me that the explanation I'd be given from my former hosts were that they were currently accommodating family, however, this He told me would have been a lie.

Three days later when the dust of my departure had not even settled I received the message I'd been expecting. My former host told me that his residence was a 'family home' and I would need to make other arrangements. When I read it, I felt insulted as though he was insinuating that I was some kind of dog. That may not have been what was intended by his words, but I did not know how else to perceive that message when I'd been so welcomed into his home (intended for guests and visitors) not even a week earlier. I was not surprised of course since God had forewarned me; I just hadn't expected it to happen the way in which it did.

With all of my experiences nothing truly surprises me. I've seen the good and the bad of human beings especially those closest to me who would constantly judge and critique my choice and style of living. I have been frequently subjected to negativity about my lifestyle, and my obedience to God was often questioned because I did not 'work.'

Sadder still is an extreme test of endurance when I had foolishly travelled to Ghana for three months, for a trip that I did not believe had God's 'full blessing.' Unlike the strangers who had hosted me in the past I was at the complete mercy of my mother who I felt controlled me.

I had absolutely no money of my own and few personal possessions which made me completely reliant on her. That was the first time as an adult that I had ever been in such a position and I hated every minute of it. I felt like I had to beg for water or beg for food which (unbeknownst to her) was not something I was used to doing.

Despite the way that I live my life and the unmerited favor I continually receive; my mum (and much of my family) held the false belief that I beg people. This is very far from the truth and is quite frankly nonsensical since begging someone does not guarantee a positive response.

The way that she treated me made me feel as though I was begging, rather than being blessed by a family member. It was then that I vowed to never put myself in such a position ever again.

Being without gas (to cook) for two days, going to bed without dinner, and surviving on an apple, pineapple and a grapefruit for the entire day just didn't seem right. Although I was in Africa, living like that made me dislike the country even more since I've had much better experiences in more impoverished parts of the world because of the kindness of strangers.

The lesson that I learnt once again was never to rely on anyone including family! Instead, I rested assured that God would provide and that the greatest kindness I would receive would probably come from a complete stranger, as it often had before.

Now my hope is that all of these stories of financial provision have not misled you into believing that God is my accountant. In fact, the blessings I have received are not only monetary, but included companionship, accommodation, transport, makeshift tour guides when I was lost, food, clothing etc. Over the past six years aside from the bout of shingles I experienced I never fell ill to the point that I required medical assistance. I believe that God will continue to look out for me, make provision and take care of all the minor details in my life.

People who argue over the authenticity of the Bible would lose an argument involving the story of my life. My experiences could not be chalked up to a fairy tale or myth; they are all true and could be easily verified for legitimacy.

I do not believe it is anyone's place to convert except Jesus therefore I do not go around trying to convert people; neither do I carry my Bible around or a handful of Gospel tracts. Although I call myself a freelance missionary, I am more of a story teller. I would share my story of living without an income for the past six years and that story always led back to Jesus. It is not so much the way I live my life and the unconventional things that I do but it is the continual flow of provision and the doors that open.

I have had an amazing journey throughout the past six years and although always riddled with challenges I never once lost sight of God's continual blessings. That is not to say that it hasn't sometimes been really hard to the point where I wanted to call it quits and meet my maker - I was just never willing to selfishly take my own life. Aside from my single status that I truly hate, I am incredibly privileged in my current position in life. I have great independence, provision and an abundance of blessings. Sadly, it does not rub off by affiliation as my friends would surely tell you, but I believe that the gifts I have are available to all because they are gifts from God.

As truly amazing as my life has been thus far it simply cannot be contained in just one book, in fact since you've only received a mere snapshot of my story you'll just have to wait for the next edition for a no frills, unedited version of the past and my current present.

Human Trafficking

♦

Movies like 'Taken' (which I am unwilling to watch) leave the general public believing a lie about human trafficking and fixated on movement and illegal immigration. The result is that trafficking often takes place in our own backyard, but we do not know what we are looking at. In fact, it is quite often hidden in plain sight as is wonderfully depicted in two videos by Courage Worldwide: 'Believe in Me' and 'Call Me Family.' In those videos you see very different instances of human trafficking involving male and female white American victims.

Every opportunity I have I show those two videos, informing my audience that they are not music videos, nor are they for the purpose of entertainment. They are an educational tool bringing the issue of human trafficking to life, so much so that when I first watched them, I cried hysterically throughout.

'Believe in Me' depicts a girl experiencing domestic violence at the hand of her father. She runs away from home and finds herself leaving one bad situation and ending up in something a lot worse. This is a sad reality because usually within the first 12 to 24-hours after running away from home that boy or girl is 'rescued' by a trafficker or pimp.

'Call Me Family' shows a girl aged seven being handed over to an old guy whilst her mother waits on the street corner in a short skirt and fishnet tights for a 'customer.' At age eight the little girl is on a merry-go-round and an older lady is grooming her before the girl is led away by the hand of an older guy. When the girl turns sixteen instead of being at prom with her peers she awaits a 'customer' who has sex with her inside her bedroom. Then when she is twenty-six she gets a phone call from the lady from the merry-go- round. A short while after a car turns up and the girl gets into the car because she has begun prostituting herself.

Disappointingly, the vast majority of people (usually aged over sixteen) believed that the girl was going off with her father or grandfather and that when she gets into the car at twenty-six, it was again her father. More recently however, I got some very strange responses that she was hitchhiking or trying to escape, neither of which made any sense but as the saying goes, 'common sense isn't common.'

The worrying thing is that many adults perceived the video as depicting something completely innocent, whilst most children under sixteen were immediately aware of the sexual nature and undertones that were overtly present. This further solidified the great need for my presentations and even more so the value that those two videos have.

'Call Me Family' begins by showing a child being sold for sex at age seven. When a girl or boy experiences trauma at a young age they become vulnerable. That vulnerability places a target on their back that is easily identified by pimps, traffickers and abusers. Similarly, there are instances when a woman would continually date abusive men as though these women gave off a fragrance or an aroma and the men could smell it, because why did every boyfriend beat them up?

Often the unwritten consensus is that victims have an invisible sign on their forehead. Hence when they attracted certain relationships it was because that sign was identified by individuals with an exploitative nature. Even in the absence of that sign the way that we dress, talk and act gives people an impression of us whether rightly or wrongly.

Modern technology particularly the ability to take selfie photographs and post them on social media sites enables a wider network of people to see us and our private lives. When a girl takes bikini shots or other sexualized or provocative photos it would lead the viewer to believe that she is sexually active or promiscuous even if that is very far from the truth.

Regardless of the security features on social media sites, photos can easily get into the hands of the wrong person such as a trafficker or pimp who would entice the presumably sexually active girl into prostitution by simply suggesting have sex for money.

There are pimps and traffickers who trail social media sites with the sole intention of picking up girls and boys for sex. That revelation is not designed to instill fear but to make you more selective about the photos that you share and the information that you post.

Pimps and traffickers are looking for vulnerability so by posting the problems you are having with your parents, boyfriend/girlfriend or spouse online this creates an opening for them to approach and console you. The anonymity of the internet enables them to take on any age, gender and ethnicity. Therefore, the girl of fourteen you believe you are talking too may instead be a 65-year-old male or femaletrafficker. As far-fetched as this seems this is a reality that happens far too many times.

Since cyber-sex trafficking is not just an issue in the Philippines but also elsewhere around the world anyone can fall prey to the unscrupulous individuals who are hidden behind a computer or cell phone screen. In fact, a friend shared with me the story of a man in America who misrepresented himself as a female scouting agent looking for minor girls to sign up to modeling agencies. He would ask them to send semi-nude or nude photos and once he received them would discontinue all communication.

The sad reality is that such a story is not uncommon. Sadder still is the naivety of such girls who are duped into sending sexual imagery of themselves over the internet all in a desperate bid to become famous. The world of the internet and dark web mean that those photos can never truly be recovered and can reappear unannounced later on in life.

Knowledge is power, and I believe that my contributions to the nation of Trinidad and Tobago have been extremely timely and valuable. My aim is to dispel the myths surrounding human trafficking moving people's focus away from illegal immigration and instead to the reality facing domestic victims including some of the many local women seen standing on street corners.

With words thrown around like sex work and conversations about the legalization of prostitution, society often holds the firm but ignorant belief that prostitution is a job and one of the oldest professions in the book. For many activists in the anti-trafficking world prostitution was never a job but was always slavery, the commoditization of one human being for the pleasure of another.

I have never once believed that prostitution is a job and after having read Rachel Moran's book, 'Paid For,' my opinion is further solidified. I do not believe prostitution is a job but if it was a job why was it only for adults? When I started work aged fifteen, I was too young to become a prostituted person. Irrespective of my own personal experience of being abused, if I had decided that I wanted to engage in 'sex work' I would have been far too young.

Now, my understanding of university is that it is a place to study for a degree and once that degree has been acquired the graduate becomes eligible for work. Typically speaking there isn't an age restriction concerning when a person can begin employment as an employer is generally swayed by the individual's qualification and not their age.

Surprisingly, despite society's perception that prostitution is a job I am perplexed by the absence of a booth and signup sheet at colleges and universities for those students who envision becoming a prostituted person. Additionally, although it does not require a degree or qualification for participation, in most parts of the West this 'profession' is illegal for anyone aged below eighteen.

Aside from this minimum age of entry, many prostituted individuals require drugs and alcohol to perform their so- called 'duties.' How many jobs require drugs and alcohol to be consumed for the completion of duties? None, but of course there may be some smart individuals who would point to the use of narcotics by celebrities, however, those substances are illegal, and are not a contractual requirement for their roles as an actor or musician.

When people call prostitution a job that would infer that the person getting the service is a customer, and if they are a customer, does that make the prostituted individual the product? In my opinion the customer is a rapist and it is paid rape every time. Many prostituted individuals are brutalized, kidnapped, raped and murdered but it somehow still constitutes a job.

The transaction often (but doesn't always) take place in a room with a bed. Is that bedroom considered to be a workplace and the bed a workstation? How can we consider a bedroom to be a workplace and a bed the workstation for any individual on this earth?

The frustrating thing I have found is that when people throw around the word, 'sex work' or 'job' in relation to prostitution, you do not see them, or their family members 'employed' in that capacity. My question is, "If prostitution is a job, why aren't you doing it? Why isn't your mum doing it? Why isn't your sister or your daughter doing it?"

It's interesting that this is the one 'job' that discriminates against your own family. When your children grow up, they can be a doctor, lawyer or bus driver - but prostitution, nope! You'd tell yourself, "That's a job for the illegal immigrants."

What people fail to realize besides the fact that prostitution isn't a job, is that human trafficking does not only involve illegal immigrants. Therefore, this book is intentionally not dealing with the trafficking of foreign nationals because the reality is that the vast majority of victims are trafficked in their home country where they look the same, dress the same, speak the same language and could easily move around undetected.

Too much focus has been given to the removal of passports and other documentation that people are not seeing the trafficking victims' right in their very own neighborhood because all they see is prostitution and what is often perceived as a way to make easy money. In my opinion that is a complete myth. Having sex with fat, old, ugly, dirty, smelly individuals is not easy money. The men and women in the sex industry have to lie for a living, they would call out, "Handsome, handsome." The guy wasn't handsome, and he knew it. After all, handsome men don't need to pay for sex because women would throw themselves at them.

Having spent countless nights in the Red-Light District between the hours of 10 p.m. and 5 a.m.. I have seen and heard a lot. I heard stories from both men and women and after seeing interactions between the prostituted men and women and their 'customers,' I am of the firm opinion that prostitution is never a job. On one occasion I observed a man with a prostituted female, it was about 11 p.m. and the guy had a walking stick. In my mind it was past his bed time, and he should have been in his bed, by himself. It was a funny situation to look at, but truth be told it really wasn't funny, it was simply disgusting.

Prostitution is so inexplicably linked with the trafficking of persons the latter of which is defined as:

"harboring, transporting, providing, or obtaining a person for compelled labor or commercial sex acts through the use of force, fraud, or coercion .... including involuntary servitude, slavery or practices similar to slavery, debt bondage, and forced labor .... Human trafficking can include but does not require movement. People may be considered trafficking victims regardless of whether they were born into a state of servitude, were transported to the exploitative situation, previously consented to work for a trafficker, or participated in a crime as a direct result of being trafficked. At the heart of this phenomenon is the traffickers' goal of exploiting and

enslaving their victims and the myriad coercive and deceptive practices they use to do so."[79]

The challenge with the legal definition is that the layman generally does not understand it aside from the word movement. Therefore, that is one of the first things people talk about, movement between countries instead of the real issue concerning the exploitation of domestic males and females.

Society now has to accept the fact that slavery no longer discriminates based on the color of a person's skin because slaves come in different colors, shapes, sizes and ethnicities. That reality still has not been accepted by a lot of people who are unwilling to wrap their head around the fact that absolutely anyone could be trafficked, and not just for sexual exploitation.

In India there are children as young as five working in rug factories. In my opinion if a child aged five serves a purpose for labor exploitation, even more so would a man or woman aged fifty or sixty who is presumably much more capable than a 5-year-old. A lot of people are unwilling to accept this as a reality and on one radio interview in particular the viewers tried their best at tearing me to shreds with their unsavory remarks. I found the entire thing incredibly humorous because they were speaking from a position of ignorance having not been to the countries I'd visited and therefore not having any of my experiences.

---

[79] U.S. Department of State, Diplomacy in Action. "Definitions and Methodology", Accessed August 25, 2018. https://www.state.gov/j/tip/rls/ tiprpt/2013/210543 htm

In the Philippines I met prostituted women who were in their late fifties and women in their late sixties who were pimps. How effective they were as pimps is another story but that was their 'vocation' for want of a better word.

But what exactly is a pimp? In those instances, I believe those women were prostituted in their younger years, and when they aged out of 'marketability' they took on the role of a pimp. This may be difficult for most people to get their head around because they are probably more familiar with an outrageously dressed black male, wearing a fur coat, plenty of gold around his neck, wrists, on his fingers and in his mouth. As is commonly assumed he is a gang lord or a drug pusher selling women for sex.

Despite how frequently the word pimp is used in mainstream society a lot of young people would mistake a pimp as purchasing women for sex instead of selling them, while adults usually assumed it was a man who sold women.

The best definition of a pimp that I received came from a 9-year-old girl in Trinidad who said, "Somebody who helps you sell your body." That summed it up really nicely because somebody could be in reference to a male or a female. The two definitions I adopted came from people in my audience:

1. Prostitute manager

2. Sexual salesman/saleswoman.

What I love about my definitions besides how short

they are is their inability to be gender specific. Pimps and traffickers could be male or female, young or old; they could be parents, friends, classmates, and even neighbors. In other words, they could be the people that you trust and least expect.

They would sometimes exhibit tremendous patience, grooming you for anything between six months to a year. You could be in a relationship and believe the other person is your boyfriend or girlfriend when in fact they are simply your future pimp, you just don't know it. Pimps and traffickers use whatever 'currency' necessary to get you to become putty in their hands. If you need someone to confide in that would be the pimp's currency; if you desire money and clothing, that would be the pimp's currency; if you need transport that would be the pimp or trafficker's currency.

During the early part of 2018 I did a television interview on the Christian station 'ACTN The Voice.' The program was live between the hours of 5 p.m. and 6 p.m. following which I was driven to a church for a presentation. When I arrived at the church a guy in the audience who had just seen me on television had been thinking, "My wife has arrived." He did not come up to me that night but started communicating with me later through Facebook. He sent me a picture of his vehicle and offered me transportation if and when I needed it.

After consulting with God, I accepted his offer of transportation for the following day. He picked me and my P.A up; dropped her off first and then proceeded to drive me home. Now normally when people drive they face forwards and focus on the road, this guy had his head turned to the left and was staring at me.

I thought I was going to die because he kept breaking suddenly. Now he wasn't young and attractive, so I really was not enjoying the attention (plus because of my insecurity I didn't like him looking at me). Then he said, "I could be a trafficker." I replied, "Well if you are a trafficker, my P.A. saw you and your license plate and the security cameras in MIC recorded you." He asked, "Is that the lawyer talking?" I replied, "Yes, it is." But everything I'd said to him was true.

Sometime later while in conversation with a friend she asked me, "Who was that Uber driver your P.A. ordered? He is not legitimate. Next time take pepper spray."

For all I knew that guy was indeed a trafficker but that day he was on strike. Irrespective of the fact that he was a stranger he had accountability. I knew the church he attended, other members of the congregation including the pastor, but God forbid if I was raped or trafficked that accountability would not have saved me.

Consider for a moment that I had known this guy for a number of years, and he was not a complete stranger. It is just as likely that he could have been a trafficker despite the length of time I had known him. If that was the case how exactly would someone safeguard themselves? I believe that the solution is communication.

Every time you enter a vehicle prepare a text message with the license plate number and the name of the driver. Alternatively, if you use a smart phone then photograph the license plate number and the person's face and say, "I'm just taking a photo of your face in case you traffic me." I'm completely serious, even if that's your great aunt.

Send that message to at least two people who genuinely care about you. Why genuinely care? There are many people in our lives who sad to say do not have our best interests at heart and would actually gloat if something bad happened to us. Then there are others who appear genuine but are seasonal and the relationship whether romantic or platonic would only be short lived.

By sending those messages, in the event that something does happen to you the police would at least know where to start their investigation. Don't ever be deceived into thinking it could never happen to you instead just take these simple but necessary precautionary steps. Finally, by announcing what you are doing when taking the picture or texting the license plate information, if that person had the intention of trafficking you, they would most definitely rethink that decision since people would know that you are with them.

I believe that aside from time, the other currency most commonly used by pimps is 'love.' This is most evident by the loyalty of their prostituted individuals, some of whom are branded. Branding is the placement of a tattoo of the pimp's name on their face or body, or other word's such as "Daddy's girl," "My property," or even a form of inscription stating their ownership to the pimp. Some of these prostituted individuals are subjected to truly horrendous treatment including threats, psychological abuse and brutal physical violence but somehow still believe the pimp loves them.

A lot of people, myself included don't really know what love is. This is despite the frequency with which we use the word when we want sex, the car keys, special privileges, money etc. I do not believe that I misuse the word love, but I would say it very easily whenever I met someone who was a blessing to me. One person that I told I loved was a new friend that I'd only met about four times and known for less than a month. So as not to scare him away I added the words in Christ and made sure he understood our friendship was strictly platonic. With the significant age gap between us there was absolutely no chance of anything beyond friendship developing but I wanted to make sure that my feelings of love were absolutely clear.

That same year on my birthday I had received over fifty Facebook well wishes. It was the first time in my life that I'd been so overwhelmed with messages that I had to take a break in responding. I made a wall post expressing my gratitude and the fact that for the first time in my life I felt loved and appreciated. My mum responded to my post by saying that I was loved but because of distractions I did not see it. I posted the response that I knew what I was saying and that my feelings were valid.

Having travelled around the world during the past six years and celebrated my birthday alone or with strangers it was the first time that I had been 'remembered.' Of course there were hundreds of my Facebook 'friends' who did not send me birthday greetings, in addition to some family members (but I chose not to dwell on that fact).

Although I would often demonstrate a hard exterior with my direct and forthright attitude I am incredibly sensitive, having built up a wall to protect myself. I am lonely and that is my vulnerability. Fortunately, I had my wits about me so I could easily avoid the snare of a trafficker, but that is not necessarily the case for a lot of other girls and women.

Please understand I do not consider myself immortal but instead I believe that I probably still have both a sign on my forehead and a target on my back; but I was doing whatever I could to protect myself despite that fact.

I love people very quickly which is often how I got hurt because I was searching for a replacement family. Whenever I saw children with two parents I envied them because it was not something I grew up with. The way I have been living my life displeases my family who out of 'genuine concern' for my safety would not provide any financial support but instead ordered me to get a paid job in England.

I am unwilling to do so because although my singleness left me unhappy, I love what I do and generally speaking I enjoy my life. As an attorney I am unwilling to move to England and get some dead-end job as a waitress or legal secretary just so I could be stable. The way I see it is that I would be earning money just to pay bills.

Now don't get me wrong I have no issue with paying bills, in fact I have been consistently paying my credit cards for the past six years, in addition to supporting my Compassion sponsored child in Ghana. My issue is that anything less than a lawyer's job in England would not progress my career as an attorney, whereas unpaid humanitarian work always does wonders to a resume.

Although I still have not obtained gainful employment in the U.S. people were impressed, so much so that I'd been invited by a judge and some lawyers for lunch. Of course, lunch does not pay the bills, but it was all part of networking.

As people frequently referred to me I am a freelance missionary, I work around the world but do not get paid. The average missionary is supported financially by their church, friends and family. I have not been supported by any one of them.

I did not ask for much because in a country like India if my family each clubbed together $15.00 once a month that would be more than enough for me to live off. On the other hand, if each member of my church gave $2.00 once a month this too would be enough for me to sustain myself. Instead all I have received is prayer which is important and has its purpose, but like someone once told me, "Give prayer legs."

To the outside observer my life is dangerous and there is the real risk that I could be trafficked, however, I believe that because of God's protection I could easily move between countries undetected. I no longer have a home anymore and even when I did going back to England was never an option.

Unlike families in India I feel like a guest in my own country. It has been so long since I actually lived there that I feel like an outsider. I no longer have a strong British accent or place of abode and once when I asked a family member for a place to spend the night I was told that I needed to give advance notice. I made a joke out of it that I didn't know advance notice was necessary to sleep on a couch but experiences like that really hurt.

1 Corinthians 13:4-8 says *"Love is:*

- *Patient*
- *Kind*
- *Does not*
    - o *Envy*
    - o *Boast*
    - o *Dishonor others*
- *Not*
    - o *Rude*
    - o *Self-seeking*
    - o *Easily angered*
- *Keeps no record of wrongs*
- *Does not delight in evil*
- *Rejoices with the truth*
- *Always*

- o   *Protects*
- o   *Trusts*
- o   *Hopes*
- o   *Perseveres"*[80]

Whenever I would ask my audience to define love they always responded with words like "Caring, a strong feeling, attraction or emotion." The sad reality is that none of these were love, and even when a strong feeling faded, that love could still remain. What was sadder still is when I would ask a church congregation to define love and they would give me those very same responses. It was incredibly rare for me to receive the correct response to my question because although some members of the audience usually knew it, it was not their reality of love.

Many parents do what my mother does that is to remind me what I did five or more years ago. That is called keeping a record of wrongs and is not loving. On the other hand, when I would remind her of what she did twenty minutes ago she'd say that it was in the past. For those of you who are parents please quit it, it's not loving, just let it go, whether or not you are Christian let the past stay in the past.

Love in Mexico takes on a whole new meaning however, whereby a group of pimps would meet a woman, date and groom her for years, before marrying her for

---

[80] *Supra 62*

the purpose of pimping her out.[81] She would believe that she had to feed her children and provide for the household, when in fact her husband was her pimp.

There are other pimps however that simply do not have the time for grooming because of how lengthy a process it can be. For these pimps and traffickers without the necessary patience to groom their victim, they would resort to using brute force, gang rape, keeping their victim in a closet without food or water for days, and then turning them out into prostitution.

Some pimps attend pimp school; get pimp certified and even read books on Pimping. One group of pimps I heard about when arrested were found with a book on slavery. In my mind I believe that's because they wanted to learn how to enslave the minds of their men and women, why else did they have a book on slavery?

In my opinion back in slave days; not the current slave days; but the days when slaves were black or brown, I believe that the men and women could not have had their hands and feet chained to effectively do their jobs. How would they have effectively cut down coffee beans and cocoa beans if their hands were chained? Quite simply, they could not.

Many modern-day slaves walk among us attending church, going to school or college, and engaging in gainful employment. They are not restricted by physical

---

[81] Siddharth, Kara. (2009) "Sex Trafficking Inside the business of modern slavery". Columbia University Press: 9

chains, so we have no idea that they are in bondage, suffering in a mental prison. Accepting this as the reality is scary for so many of us, because it means that we come into contact with victims of human trafficking all the time, but simply don't know it.

In my opinion whenever you have men and women and sex, you have sex trafficking. In my opinion, whenever you have restaurants, businesses and establishments you have labor trafficking, and in my opinion whenever you have sick people, people with ailments, you have organ trafficking. In my opinion human trafficking takes place everywhere in the world and is often a lot closer to home than we perceive.

Signs and Symptoms of Human Trafficking

♦

Identifying a trafficking victim requires knowledge of certain indicators particularly when the victim is a native of the country in which they are trafficked and therefore a passport or other documentation would not be seized.

Behavior or Characteristics in Pimps/Traffickers:

- "Jealous, controlling and violent
- Significantly older than female companions
- Promises things that seem too good to be true
- Encourages victims to engage in illegal activities to achieve their goals and dreams
- Buys expensive gifts or owns expensive items
- Is vague about his/her profession
- Pushy or demanding about sex
- Encourages inappropriate sexual behavior
- Makes the victim feel responsible for his/her financial stability. Very open about financial matters."[82]

---

[82] Shared Hope International, "Report Trafficking", Accessed August 30, 2018. https://sharedhope.org/join-the-cause/report-trafficking/

Warning Signs in a Trafficked Individual:

- "Signs of physical abuse such as burn marks, bruises or cuts
- Unexplained absences from class
- Less appropriately dressed than before
- Sexualized behavior
- Overly tired in class
- Brags about making or having lots of money
- Displays expensive clothes, accessories or shoes
- Shows signs of gang affiliation? (i.e. a preference for specific colors, notebook doodles of gang symbols, etc."[83]
- Sleeping on the work premises
- Branding (a tattoo of a name, bar-code)
- Is not free to leave or come and go as he/she wishes
- Is under 18 and is providing commercial sex acts
- Is in the commercial sex industry and has a pimp/ manager
- Is unpaid, paid very little, or paid only through tips
- Works excessively long and/or unusual hours
- Is not allowed breaks or suffers under unusual restrictions at work
- Owes a large debt and is unable to pay it off
- Was recruited through false promises concerning the nature and conditions of his/her work
- High security measures exist in the work and/or

---

[83] Shared Hope International, "Report Trafficking", Accessed August 30, 2018. https://sharedhope.org/join-the-cause/report-trafficking/

living locations (e.g. opaque windows, boarded up windows, bars on windows, barbed wire, security cameras, etc.)

- Is fearful, anxious, depressed, submissive, tense, or nervous/paranoid
- Exhibits unusually fearful or anxious behavior after bringing up law enforcement
- Avoids eye contact
- Lacks health care
- Appears malnourished
- Shows signs of physical and/or sexual abuse, physical restraint, confinement, or torture
- Has few or no personal possessions
- Is not in control of his/her own money, no financial records, or bank account
- Is not in control of his/her own identification documents (ID or passport)
- Is not allowed or able to speak for themselves (a third party may insist on being present and/or translating)
- Claims of just visiting and inability to clarify where he/she is staying/address
- Lack of knowledge of whereabouts and/or do not know what city he/she is in
- Loss of sense of time
- Has numerous inconsistencies in his/her story
- This list is not exhaustive and represents only a selection of possible indicators."[84]

---

[84] Polaris, "Recognize The Signs", Accessed August 30, 2018. https:// polarisproject. org/human-trafficking/recognize-signs

Concluding Thoughts

◆

As a survivor of childhood sexual abuse I understand firsthand the tremendous importance of giving a voice to the issues that are more often than not kept secret and hidden. No one wants to talk about the elephant in the room, but by not doing so the cycle of abuse will continue generation after generation.

Telling my story is my way of connecting with other victims and survivors. I, figuratively speaking get down inside the pit and meet them where they are instead of standing at the top shouting down my sympathy, care and concern. This is the way empathy should look, actually joining a person and journeying alongside them in their pain and continuing throughout their healing.

Instead of being judgmental or comparing experiences, I would continually use my story as a means to inspire the people in the room that their past does not have to dictate their future. I made the decision to become vulnerable through my transparency.

After living in secret for decades I am finally able to experience some semblance of freedom. My story has inspired people and I believe that every life could be a source of inspiration to at least one other individual. As I shared earlier we all make mistakes, some with more devastating effects than others, but I believe that we all have the capacity to do something positive in our lives whether we chose to do so or not.

My desire to write this book was two-fold. I wanted to expand on my coined tagline of "Can you keep a secret?" and ensure that audience members never again had to leave my presentations empty handed. Instead I wanted to equip them with a valuable source of information that would recap the material discussed. As sad as this is to say, I want parents and caregivers to have a manual with a checklist of signs and identifiers that would help them establish if a child had indeed been a victim of childhood sexual abuse or human trafficking.

The sad reality is that there are simply never enough hours in a day for me to be able to share everything I know with a room full of people. Plus, as society constantly changes and evolves there are always new developments, the occasional amendments in law and greater depravity and deviance in the sexual crimes that occur.

Typically, my presentations are two hours but could very easily last up to three without Q&A. For those individuals who have never heard me speak they were often daunted by that duration. They frequently doubted my ability to engage the audience and retain their attention for an extended period of time. This is most likely based on inaccurate assumptions and past experiences. I, however, always have complete confidence in delivering my presentations to a room full of people irrespective of the number of participants. I have no doubt that I have a God given gift which guarantees that my audience were always enraptured to the point that they often lost sense of time.

I have often been amused when the audience's response shocked even the program organizer who had been privy to my presentation in the past but still did not have full confidence in the success of my delivery. This happened on a number of occasions when my presentation had gone over the allocated time but no one in the audience had even noticed. Since I closely observed my audience I never ceased to be amazed by their attentiveness and willingness to learn. Outside of my presentations people loved to make the obvious statement that I talk a lot, or rather that I talk too much. During my presentations from the affirmative reactions that I consistently received, I felt almost as though I had not talked enough.

My presentations are not lectures although they were often incorrectly referred to as such. They were conversations requiring active audience participation. Some people referred to my talks as a session on awareness. However, in my opinion awareness is a dirty word because it involves knowing about an issue but doing nothing, e.g. "John across the road sells drugs." To which you would respond, "I'm aware." That would be it, nothing more, nothing less. A statement of fact was made, and you acknowledged your awareness of it but had no intention of doing anything about what you heard. For this reason, I place a great deal of emphasis on the words education and empowerment which means educating someone and empowering them with the tools to act.

As a visionary (and somewhat freelance missionary) I envision in Trinidad and Tobago a time not too far away in the future when all the nation's people have been educated and empowered on the concept of "Can you keep a secret?" I believe that provided I have done my job effectively and people have retained the information they received, then the result would be that every time that question is asked, the answer would always be an unequivocal, "Yes." By responding in the affirmative the other individual would subsequently disclose their secret and therefore be able to get the help that they need to enable them to be removed from a negative or abusive situation or environment.

As I type the above I have a great reluctance in doing so because there is not an adequate system in place to safeguard and protect the country's victims. There is a common belief amongst locals that the police and authority figures are corrupt. The nation's people have no faith in their government sometimes to the detriment of themselves or others, particularly with regards to reporting crime. People often fear that their safety would be jeopardized, and that if they disclose knowledge of a crime the perpetrators' would silence them. This fear is not unfounded in many cases, but I am saddened by the reality that a person's selfishness in protecting themselves from danger indirectly allows a victim to continue to be victimized. On the other hand, when the authorities are indeed notified and get involved in a case of abuse, often times the child is returned back to the abusive environment or in the rare case that they are placed in a children's home they are once again subjected to abuse.

My opinions on this issue are simply that we have a responsibility to do the right thing for the Daisy in our world. We need to notify the authorities that an abusive situation exists and allow them to do their job. Worst case scenario and they are indeed corrupt; at least you did your part to protect the victim. The alternative is to believe that the police are corrupt and say nothing to them. In my opinion, even if they are indeed corrupt, I believe that because of the power of God, the day you inform the police of an abusive situation, would be the same day they decide not to be corrupt. As far-fetched as this may sound I believe that anything is possible.[85]

Society's lack of faith in the people who hold a position of power is a huge issue in Trinidad. That is also notwithstanding the fact that many individuals have an island mentality, they do not want to get involved in other people's business in the event that they get dragged in to the proceedings.

I come from a completely different culture where I do not have any of the concerns that the people in Trinidad experience. Despite that I do understand that it is not a

---

[85] *"With men this is impossible; but with God all things are possible."* Matthew 19:26 (KJV)

safe country, but I am unwilling to be overtaken with fear or paranoia. Some people would disagree with me because of the mere fact that I do not take public transportation in either of the two islands, and do not leave my house unless accompanied or with a safe, reputable driver. The result as I would often say is that if I did not speak (on human trafficking) not only did I not eat but I did not leave my house. The result was that I stayed indoors like a prisoner.

Human trafficking is a multi-billion-dollar criminal industry, a subject that really isn't up for much discussion in Trinidad and Tobago hence why the residents are in denial of its existence there. During the previous year I had made so many media appearances on the T.V., radio and in newspapers that I lost count. My face and voice are known which make me a target. Fortunately, I have yet to capture the attention of the unscrupulous individuals in the criminal underworld, but it would only be a matter of time before they perceived me as an actual threat to their 'business.'

My 'prison' way of surviving in Trinidad and Tobago is a necessity until the day that National Security identifies my value and the safety risks surrounding me and provides me with much needed police escort and transportation. Until then I take every precautionary measure to ensure that I do not return home in a body bag.

I would jump at every opportunity to present on human trafficking which gave some individuals the mistaken belief that speaking is my life. They would be wrong, Jesus is my life, speaking is just my 'hobby.'

Concluding Thoughts

As I once shared with a friend, "I am not a speaker because I've only been speaking for a total of about forty days." This was probably very close to the truth, because although I had not actually counted the number of speaking engagements I'd had, it really hadn't been that many. Consequently I want to use this opportunity to advertise my global availability for speaking engagements on human trafficking. More information can be found by visiting my website: changingcases.org; or you can certainly reach out to me via e-mail: Juanita.headley@changingcases.com; or visit my Facebook page: Changing Cases.

I do NOT charge for my presentations because I deem it inappropriate to charge people to be educated and empowered on the issues discussed here in this book but to sustain the work that I do the collection of a suggested donation has become mandatory, however, there are always exceptions to the rule so please don't allow that fact to deter you. At the end of the day no organization or its volunteers can survive on positive reviews alone as expenses are incurred for things as simple as transportation to presentations.

I speak to any size audience with an age preference of nine years and above. This is a message not aimed just at children but at people of all ages since absolutely anybody could become a victim of exploitation.

During one summer I was thrown into the deep end at some camps in Trinidad and Tobago where my audience included children as young as five. Common sense took over, so I tailored my presentation accordingly and although it was a job well done I really shy away from such young audiences.

One of the challenges with very young children is the need to explain a lot of basic words which takes away precious time from the entire presentation. I will say however, that when I have had children aged nine participate in my presentation they often gave more educated responses than most adults, which is not necessarily because of personal experience.

The bigger issue however is a safety concern. These education and empowerment talks bring knowledge and with that greater protection. With greater knowledge, fewer boys and girls would be abused and exploited which would directly impact the pockets of pimps and traffickers. I am shaking up the hornets' nest by trying to destroy a thriving criminal industry. Therefore, I and anyone else in the fight against trafficking are considered a problem and I know this better than most people because many of my friends have received death threats and attempts made on their lives.

Having met countless survivors of childhood sexual abuse I can say with a great deal of confidence and certainty that most victims of abuse are abused under the age of ten. Bearing this fact in mind, if I brought my presentation to a class full of 10-year-olds, there is guaranteed to be a victim or victims right in that room.

Now consider a scenario where I spoke to one hundred children and fifty of them confessed to being abused. How would the teachers handle that? There is no system in place to deal with such a huge number of disclosures all at the same time. Are there even enough spaces in children's home? And if there isn't then those children would be returned home and continue to be the subject of sexual abuse.

My biggest concern is that if I visited primary schools and there were disclosures of abuse made but no intervention for whatever reason, that child would go back home to the abusive situation and probably think, "What was the point in saying anything? Nothing has been done. I should have just kept quiet, it's my fault anyway." Consequently, when that child becomes an adult and enters into an abusive relationship, it would simply be their normal because they had been conditioned by their earlier experience. They would probably think as many victims often do, "My dad abused me sexually and no one did anything about it, my boyfriend is abusive, but I deserve it. Everyone in my world just takes advantage of me."

To those of you who do not understand how prevalent sexual abuse and incest are this may sound incredibly far-fetched but I believe that my concerns are completely reasonable and valid. When a child is at a young age they process things very differently from adults. They are in a season of learning, and that learning would or would not be destructive.

Therefore, as hard as this is for me to say, I would much rather talk to those children who have survived abuse, than those currently going through it because I have no faith in the system in Trinidad and Tobago to do the right thing, not because of corruption but simply lack of resources. I feel very similarly about England however, because although I believe that the correct system is in place, there are simply not enough beds for victims. The result is that those children would be taken to foster homes where they are often subjected yet again to sexual abuse.

This is a very sad reality even more so when considering the fact that there are unscrupulous individuals who seek out adoption or fostering as a means for them to access and engage in sexual activity with children. One such individual who was arrested for manufacturing and possessing child pornography had been researching on his home computer what would happen to him if he sexually abused his adopted children.[86] The man had no adopted children at the time, but he had certainly wanted them. When I read this article, I made an addition to my prayer list and began praying for foster and adopted children.

A few years later I read an article on Facebook about two gay men with an adopted son, who were in the process of adopting a second son. In the process of the second adoption it was uncovered that these men had been sexually abusing son number one from the time he was one until they were caught when he was aged six.[87]

---

[86] "Salem Man Arrested On Child Pornography Charges" *WMUR 9*, November 11 2015. http://www.wmur.com/news/salem-man-arrested-on-child- pornography-charges-police-say/36360818

[87] Kate Darvall, "Depraved Gay Pedophile Couple Who Adopted A Boy And Shared Him With A Child Sex Ring For Six Years Were Trying to 'Buy' A Second Child To Abuse When They Were Arrested", *The Daily Mail*, November 16, 2017.http://www.dailymail.co.uk/news/article-5087453/ Cairns-gay-couple-Mark-Newton-Peter-Truong.html

When I read that article I told myself, that was why I had begun praying for the protection of children who were in the adoption and foster care system. Their safety is important but so is mine and I am concerned for my personal safety.

Now imagine a situation where I am educating primary school children on abuse and a disclosure is made about a father. What would happen when that father arrives to pick up his child from school?

Traffickers and pimps want to take out every anti-trafficking activist but what about if I get into the family situation? I know how vicious women can be particularly in the Caribbean where if you are trying to involve yourself with their man they would throw acid on you or worse. What about if that father was the bread winner and the mother knew about the abuse and had simply turned a blind eye (as is often the case)?

I am not willing to put myself into any more danger than I already have. Travelling around the country without police escort, being hosted by friends of friends all place me at risk. I am willing to make certain sacrifices because I am so passionate about my ministry, but that should not include sacrificing my own life - after all who would take up my baton if I was no longer here? Right now, the list of individuals willing to follow in my footsteps is nil.

As people would not stop telling me, I have a calling on my life, a God given ministry. I believe that they are right because if I indeed had a choice I would not have chosen to live the last six years in a wholly unpaid capacity. As I would often say, "No normal person volunteers six years for free, living like a gypsy, unless they are crazy, or something is driving them. For me, Jesus is the driving force behind what I do, and it is my faith in Him which leads to my life of obedience."

I live on a different playing field to most Christians, I live by faith and the last six years demonstrates that fact. As the Bible says, *"Now faith is the substance of things hoped for, the evidence of things not seen."*[88]

I do not have blind faith, but my faith is in a God that has proved Himself faithful to me time and time again. Is living like a Christian easy? No, it isn't, and the Bible never said it would be. My life is a living testimony of an amazing God who I don't always see eye to eye with but despite all of the challenges He allows me to experience I could never deny how truly blessed I am.

In faith I am writing this book with the belief that I have been blessed with a publisher who will take my book all throughout the world to places that I could never reach by myself. In faith I believe that I will be blessed to get married one day, and my prayer is that it would be 'soon.' Please understand it has nothing to do with marital sex, in fact as a result of the abuse I went through I have no interest in sex (which is completely understandable). For me marriage unlocks the door for me to finally adopt two Filipino street children. In faith I believe that I will adopt and have an orphanage

---

[88] *Supra 24*

in the Philippines, and in faith I believe that I will have my Nonprofit open hiring policy bakery.

My life is full of so many unaccomplished dreams, but I believe that in God's perfect timing they would indeed become a reality. My desire is that this book inspires you, that despite the journey of my life being what many describe as unique that the theme you saw throughout is that I am simply an ordinary person blessed to do extraordinary things; and therefore, you too could accomplish anything you set out to do. As I shared earlier, your past does not have to dictate your future. It really isn't how you start the race but how you finish that counts.

God bless you!!

Appendix: Path to Salvation

After all my talk of God I believe that this book would be incomplete without allowing you, the reader, the opportunity to invite Him into your life and embark on your very own personal journey with Him. Please allow me to explain because I accept and acknowledge that there are many gods, and many lords, however, the God I am referring to is written about in the King James (not the Queen James) Bible, and the Lord I am referencing is His son, Lord Jesus Christ.

I have been a church attendee my entire life but made a personal commitment to give my life to Christ at the age of sixteen. Although I was young and impressionable at the time, I was taken through a Biblical study course and entered into the waters of baptism fully informed of the decision that I had made. I have never looked back since.

Now, aside from the small matter of being unhappily single I am incredibly blessed and although I believe that I am God's favorite, you too could be because truth be told He actually doesn't have any favorites. Favoritism aside, first a moment of disclosure; I cannot guarantee that you will have the luxury of travelling to six or more countries a year on $10.00 flight tickets. Nor can I guarantee that you'll be overwhelmed with financial provision and the kindness of strangers.

What I can guarantee is that you will have life more abundantly.[89]

Please understand however, that life may come with greater challenges than those you previously experienced[90] because God never promised the Christian walk would be a bed of roses. What He does promise is eternity[91] with Him. He is an inclusive God[92] allowing everyone the opportunity to become His sons and daughters.[93] Unlike the world that advocates abortion and the death penalty, He is a God of second chances and advocates we likewise forgive others too.[94]

Forgiveness is available to you today.[95] There is no magic to giving your life to Christ, there isn't even a script it's simply a heart[96] decision.

Three of the most common steps to becoming a Christian are as easy as *ABC*:

---

[89] *"I am come that they might have life, and that they might have it more abundantly."* John 10:10 (KJV)

[90] *"Do not be afraid of what you are about to suffer. I tell you, the devil will put some of you in prison to test you."* Revelation 2:10 (NIV)

[91] *"Whoever hears my word and believes Him who sent me has eternal life and will not be judged but has crossed over from death to life."* John 5:24 (NIV)

[92] *"Jesus answered, "I am the way and the truth and the life. No one comes to the Father except through me."* John 14:6 (NIV)

[93] *"And, I will be a Father to you, and you will be my sons and daughters, says the Lord Almighty."* 2 Corinthians 6:18 (NIV)

[94] *Supra 2; "Forgive us our debts, as we also have forgiven our debtors."* Matthew 6:12 (NIV)

[95] *Supra 47*

[96] *"If you declare with your mouth, "Jesus is Lord", and believe in your heart that God raised him from the dead, you will be saved. For it is with your heart that you believe and are justified, and it is with your mouth that you profess your faith and are saved."* Romans 10:9-10 (NIV)

Appendix: Path to Salvation

Admit that you are a sinner, apologize to God for all the sins you have committed and turn away from your sinful lifestyle.

Verses that support this step:

> "For all have sinned, and come short of the glory of God." Romans 3:23 (KJV)

> "For the wages of sin is death; but the gift of God is eternal life through Jesus Christ our Lord." Romans 6:23 (KJV)

> "Repent then, and turn to God, so that your sins may be wiped out, that times of refreshing may come from the Lord."Acts 3:19 (NIV)

> "If we confess our sins, He is faithful and just and will forgive us our sins and purify us from all unrighteousness." 1 John 1:9 (NIV)

Believe that Jesus is the Son of God who died to pay the penalty for your sins.

Verses discussing belief:

> "For God so loved the world, that He gave His only begotten Son, that whosoever believeth in Him should not perish but have everlasting life." John 3:16 (KJV)

> "Jesus answered, "I am the way and the truth and the life. No one comes to the Father except through me." John 14:6 (NIV)

> "But God demonstrates His own love for us in this:

While we were still sinners, Christ died for us."
Romans 5:8 (NIV)

Confess your faith in Jesus Christ as your Lord and Savior

Read:

> *"If you declare with your mouth, "Jesus is Lord",*
> *and believe in your heart that God raised him from*
> *the dead, you will be saved. For it is with your heart*
> *that you believe and are justified, and it is with your*
> *mouth that you profess your faith and are saved....*
> *Everyone who calls on the name of the Lord will be*
> *saved." Romans 10:9-10, 13 (NIV)*

Once you have completed these ABC steps you can say this prayer out loud:

> *Dear God,*
>
> *I know that I am a sinner and there is nothing*
> *that I can do to save myself. I confess my complete*
> *helplessness to forgive my own sin or to work my way*
> *to heaven. At this moment I trust Christ alone as the*
> *One who bore my sin when He died on the cross. I*
> *believe that He did all that will ever be necessary for*
> *me to stand in your holy presence. I thank you that*
> *Christ was raised from the dead as a guarantee of my*
> *own resurrection. As best as I can, I now transfer my*
> *trust to Him. I am grateful that He has promised to*
> *receive me despite my many sins and failures. Father,*
> *I take you at your word. I thank you that I can face*
> *death now that you are my Savior. Thank you for*

the assurance that you will walk with me through the deep valley. Thank you for hearing this prayer.

In Jesus' Name.

Amen.[97]

I am excited to share that you are now a Christian!!!

This is truly the best decision that you could make whether this is the first time you have decided to follow Christ, or you have just recommitted your life to Him. I would love to hear from you so that I can follow your journey, pray for you and offer any spiritual support. You can contact me via email: Juanita.headley@changingcases.com or send a friend request on Facebook: Changing Cases.

So, what's next?

You need to join a Bible believing church that teaches sound doctrine; share with other Christians the decision you have just made;[98] and discuss with the church leaders that you would like to be taken through the relevant teachings in preparation for water baptism.

Just some unsolicited advice for your new life as a Christian:

■ *Purchase a King James Version of the Bible*

---

[97] John Barnett, "The Sinners Prayer – 4 Examples for Salvation" *Crosswalk*, February 16 2017. https://www.crosswalk.com/faith/prayer/prayers/the- sinners-prayer-4-examples.html

[98] *"Whoever is ashamed of me and my words, the Son of Man will be ashamed of them..."* Luke 9:26 (NIV)

o   **Read the Bible daily**

I recommend an entire chapter in the morning and one in the evening. In doing so, you would read the entire Bible within two years. It is usually advised that new Christians should start in the New Testament, so my advice will likewise be the same.

I advocate the King James Bible because it's close to the original text. Additionally, the more modern versions omit certain words and even entire scriptures from their translation. 'The Message' is one such Bible I would strongly discourage you from purchasing because of its use of incredibly simplistic language among other things. If you do a comparison of the same scripture from the different Bible versions then you'd understand what I mean.

o   **Keep a prayer diary**

This could be any notebook where you would write the date at the top of the page and list your prayer requests below.

I have seen the power of prayer whether my eyes are open or closed. So, I know that this works. There isn't some intricate art in writing down your prayer requests; it simply enables you to keep track of everything especially when they are answered.

Specificity is crucial i.e. dates, times, month, year etc. I always start with the words, "Thank you."[99]

---

[99] *"Giving thanks always for all things unto God."* Ephesians 5:20 (KJV)

Appendix: Path to Salvation

An example of a specific prayer request that God answered for me went like this, "Thank you God that you will provide me free, clean, cockroach free, spider free, and mosquito free accommodation in a private room with full ceiling on Thursday, August 2nd, 2018." God did exactly that and more.

Whenever God answers a prayer request, place a check mark beside it and the date that He answered. This serves as a reminder and encouragement for future prayer requests.

o **Pray at least twice daily**

Before reading the Bible ask the Holy Spirit for understanding[100] and that He will speak to you through His Word. Read the Bible followed by reading your prayer requests out loud. After that you can close your eyes and pray from your heart, talk to God just as though you were having a conversation with someone close to you.

I encourage you to pray as soon as you wake up and last thing at night. The length of your prayer isn't what counts it's the sincerity of your words.

The Bible says, *"For where two or three gather in my name, there am I with them."*[101] Corporal prayer is a very beautiful thing. Not only does it allow others to come alongside you and provide that spiritual support, but it also enables more people to be

---

[100] *"Then he opened their minds so they could understand the Scriptures."* Luke 24:45 (NIV)

[101] Matthew 18:20 (NIV)

blessed by hearing your praise report because they were part of your petition.

A pastor preached once about the story of Lazarus[102] when Jesus had said, "Take away the stone."[103] For those who do not know the story, Lazarus had been ill and eventually died because Jesus delayed his visit. This was Jesus first miracle of raising the dead so His timing was impeccable.

Now considering the power that Jesus had to raise a dead body back to life, the movement of a stone from the mouth of the cave would be an easy feat. He could simply command the stone and it would move. The pastor explained that the reason Jesus asked the bystanders to move the stone was for their participation and involvement in His miracle. This can be likened to corporal prayer, when a group of people pray together they are figuratively moving the stone away allowing God the opportunity to raise the dead body.

It is recommended that men pray with men and women pray with women. Prayer is very intimate and is sometimes misused to create closeness between another individual. I know this full well because I was guilty of doing so.

In the Philippines I developed a fast friendship with a fellow Christian. We very quickly became prayer partners and would talk and pray on the

---

[102] John 11 (NIV)

[103] John 11:39 (NIV)

phone every day. Despite my improper motives I was still a recipient of answered prayers.

Unfortunately, I wanted to help God out, so I spoke to the best friend of my prayer partner telling him that I was in love and wanted him to be the facilitator in what was currently a strictly platonic relationship. That was one of the worst decisions that I could have ever made because he 'deceitfully' showed our entire Facebook conversation to my prayer partner.

I felt humiliated and violated. It was not the right time and things had not been done the right way. As a result of this my prayer partner retreated and aside from one brief phone call the following week he has not spoken to me since.

Over a year has passed since that happened, but at the time it was one of the hardest experiences I have ever endured. I have never had such a close friendship with anyone before that was solely centered on prayer. Months later my heart broke when my prayer partner blocked me on Facebook.

I believe this was the first time I was ever truly in love particularly as there was absolutely no physical attraction on my side. I experienced tremendous guilt and blame for a long time afterwards for foolishly getting his best friend involved and having him completely sabotage our relationship.

Did I learn from my experience, sadly no I didn't because I tried to get his sister involved but that failed too and probably made matters a lot worse.

The lesson to be learned here, don't get involved in God's business; instead trust that His timing and plans[104] are perfect and don't help Him out. God knows what He's doing.

o   ***Attend church every Sunday***

Locate a Bible believing church that you can become a part of and find a way to serve in one of the church ministries.

Attend the weekly meetings so that you can grow in knowledge as well as build new friendships and relationships.

A word of caution however, a lot of churches and Christian ministries are compromising the word of God, including giving false teachings. There is sadly a lot of performance in church that makes a mockery of Christianity and does not glorify God.

Two questions I always ask myself:

1.   Does it glorify God?

2.   Is it in the Bible?

Both questions can be answered by referring back to the Bible. The third question I ask myself:

1.   Did Jesus do it?

Again, the answer to that question is in the Bible.

---

[104] *"A man's heart deviseth his way: but the Lord directeth his steps."* Proverbs 16:9 (KJV)

264

Appendix: Path to Salvation

There are many manifestations taking place in churches that were not demonstrated by Jesus. Aside from speaking in tongues[105] (which is a hotly debated topic) that is written about in scripture; much of what is being seen today did not happen at any point in the Bible's history.

I do not want to stray or digress too much, but I want to make an important point about speaking in tongues in accordance with what the Bible says in 1 Corinthians 14:2- 33 (NIV):

> *"For anyone who speaks in a tongue does not speak to people but God. Indeed, no one understands them; they utter mysteries by the Spirit.... Anyone who speaks in a tongue edifies themselves, but the one who prophecies edifies the church ... I would rather have you prophesy.*
>
> *The one who prophesies is greater than the one who speaks in tongues, unless someone interprets, so that the church may be edified.... Now brothers and sisters, if I come to you and speak in tongues, what good will I be to you, unless I bring you some revelation or knowledge or prophecy or word of instruction? ... Unless you speak intelligible words with your tongue, how will anyone know what you are saying? You will just be speaking into the air.[10] Undoubtedly there are all sorts of languages in the world, yet none of*

---

[105] *"To another speaking in different kinds of tongues."* 1 Corinthians 12:10 (NIV)

them is without meaning.[11] If then I do not grasp the meaning of what someone is saying, I am a foreigner to the speaker, and the speaker is a foreigner to me.[12] So it is with you. Since you are eager for gifts of the Spirit, try to excel in those that build up the church.[13]

For this reason the one who speaks in a tongue should pray that they may interpret what they say.[14] For if I pray in a tongue, my spirit prays, but my mind is unfruitful.[15] So what shall I do? I will pray with my spirit, but I will also pray with my understanding; I will sing with my spirit, but I will also sing with my understanding.[16] Otherwise when you are praising God in the Spirit, how can someone else, who is now put in the position of an inquirer,[d] say "Amen" to your thanksgiving, since they do not know what you are saying?[17] You are giving thanks well enough, but no one else is edified.[18]

I thank God that I speak in tongues more than all of you.[19] But in the church I would rather speak five intelligible words to instruct others than ten thousand words in a tongue....

Tongues, then, are a sign, not for believers but for unbelievers; prophecy, however, is not for unbelievers but for believers.[23] So if the whole church comes together and everyone speaks in tongues, and inquirers or unbelievers come in, will they not say that you are out of your mind?[24]

But if an unbeliever or an inquirer comes in while everyone is prophesying, they are convicted of sin and are brought under judgment by all,[25] as the secrets of their hearts are laid bare. So they will fall down and worship God, exclaiming, "God is really among you!" What then shall we say, brothers and sisters? When you come together, each of you has a hymn, or a word of instruction, a revelation, a tongue or an interpretation. Everything must be done so that the church may be built up.[27] If anyone speaks in a tongue, two – or at the most three – should speak, one at a time, and someone must interpret.[28] If there is no interpreter, the speaker should keep quiet in the church and speak to himself and to God.[29]

Two or three prophets should speak, and the others should weigh carefully what is said.[30] And if a revelation comes to someone who is sitting down, the first speaker should stop.[31] For you can all prophesy in turn so that everyone may be instructed and encouraged.[32] The spirits of prophets are subject to the control of prophets.[33] For God is not a God of disorder but of peace – as in all the congregations of the Lord's people."

The Bible is clear that interpretation is mandatory whenever tongues are spoken publicly; however from my travels around the world I have only experienced the translation of tongues in one church in America. In all other churches the worship leader, pastor or others on the platform burst out in tongues whilst no one had any idea what they were saying. Just as the Bible says it is not edifying.[106] It's like if I started writing this

---

[106]   1 Corinthians 14:17 (NIV)

book in Filipino, unless you could read Tagalog the words on the page would be completely meaningless to you; likewise, in the church congregation. I do not understand why it happens with so much frequency, maybe as if to somehow signify holiness.

I do not speak in tongues and according to the Bible neither did Jesus. I believe that if speaking in tongues were as important as people make it out to be Jesus would have been doing so throughout His ministry.

Now, many of the other manifestations that are seen in churches are deeply concerning sometimes replicating demonic possession. 1 Corinthians 12:4-11 (NIV) lays out the spiritual gifts:

> *"There are different kinds of gifts, but the same Spirit distributes them.[5] There are different kinds of service, but the same Lord.[6] There are different kinds of working, but in all of them and in everyone it is the same God at work.[7]*

> *Now to each one the manifestation of the Spirit is given for the common good.[8] To one there is given through the Spirit a message of wisdom, to another a message of knowledge by means of the same Spirit,[9] to another faith by the same Spirit, to another gifts of healing by that one Spirit,[10] to another miraculous powers, to another prophecy, to another distinguishing between spirits, to another speaking in different kinds of tongues,[a] and to still another the interpretation of tongues.[b][11] All these are the work of one and the same Spirit, and he distributes them to each one, just as he determines."*

Appendix: Path to Salvation

The scripture which carries the most weight in my mind when manifestations occur can be found in Galatians 5:22 (NIV):

"But the fruit of the Spirit is love, joy, peace, forbearance, kindness, goodness, faithfulness, gentleness and self-control."

Whenever a person exhibits a lack of self-control in a 'godly' manifestation this raises serious questions in my mind. For example, if the fruit of the spirit was love, how could you demonstrate hate and say that hatred came from God?

This is just some food for thought. My opinions on this are very strong because of the warning giving in Matthew 24:4-27

"Jesus answered: "Watch out that no one deceives you.[5] For many will come in my name, claiming, 'I am the Messiah,' and will deceive many.[6] You will hear of wars and rumors of wars, but see to it that you are not alarmed. Such things must happen, but the end is still to come.[7] Nation will rise against nation, and kingdom against kingdom. There will be famines and earthquakes in various places.[8] All these are the beginning of birth pains.[9]

"Then you will be handed over to be persecuted and put to death, and you will be hated by all nations because of me.[10] At that time many will turn away from the faith and will betray and hate each other,[11] and many false prophets will appear and deceive many people.[12] Because of the increase of wickedness, the

love of most will grow cold,[13] *but the one who stands firm to the end will be saved.*[14] *And this gospel of the kingdom will be preached in the whole world as a testimony to all nations, and then the end will come....*[23]

At that time if anyone says to you, 'Look, here is the Messiah!' or, 'There he is!' do not believe it.[24] *For false messiahs and false prophets will appear and perform great signs and wonders to deceive, if possible, even the elect.*[25] *See, I have told you ahead of time.*[26]

"So if anyone tells you, 'There he is, out in the wilderness,' do not go out; or, 'Here he is, in the inner rooms,' do not believe it.27 For as lightning that comes from the east is visible even in the west, so will be the coming of the Son of Man.28"

When people told me that it is a new spirit in the church this confused me because of the scripture Hebrews 13:8 (KJV) which says, *"Jesus Christ the same yesterday, and today, and forever."* I believe that by cleverly using the word 'new' in relation to Christianity that is our way of justifying the changes that are occurring in the church. However, I have to refer to another scripture found in 1 Corinthians 14:33 (KJV) *"For God is not the author of confusion, but of peace."*

The Bible is unequivocally clear about the manifestations of God, and I have presented the information here. It is now up to you to decide whether you're going to live 100% by the Bible or be a pick and mix Christian disregarding His truths and instead allowing yourself to be swept away by what you see, feel and experience in a church setting.

Let me be clear, when I say live 100% by the Bible I mean the entire Bible, not focusing solely on the Old Testament or solely on the New Testament but applying the Bible in its entirety to your life. Please understand that I am in no way advocating legalism because I live by the scripture, *"To obey is better than sacrifice."*[107]

I want to tread very carefully here so what I will say is that God is looking at your heart[108] not your attire, the tattoos or piercings you may have, or the length and style of your hair. Sadly, some members of church congregations do exactly that, judge a person on the outside which is something I have personally experienced on a number of occasions.

In some church denominations jewelry is prohibited. I am not a rule breaker, but I am reluctant to remove my bracelets when I am merely a visiting guest or speaker. This is not my attempt at outright rebellion or disrespect, on the contrary I am willing to make necessary adjustments by wearing a skirt and ensuring my shoulders are covered but I am not comfortable with the idea of removing my bracelets. Why? They hold huge sentimental value because they are gifts from the girls and boys in the Philippines from my trips in 2014, 2017 and 2018. I wear them during T.V. interviews and

---

[107] 1 Samuel 15:22 (NIV)

[108] *"The Lord does not look at the things people look at. People look at the outward appearance, but the Lord looks at the heart."* 1 Samuel 16:7 (NIV)

presentations and although the collection continues to grow, I wear them with pride. I love those children and want them to see how much I treasure and value the gifts they gave me by not taking them off. The only exception to my rule is if wearing my bracelets would result in the cancellation of a speaking engagement, in such an instance I would indeed compromise because my message on human trafficking holds greater value then my wrist decoration.

I was talking with a friend once who explained that he had not taken communion one Sunday because the church had not practiced the washing of feet. I asked him, "If you went to another country and they didn't wash feet. Would you take communion?" He responded negatively. Having travelled to twenty-nine countries and been to different churches and denominations I have never seen or experienced that practice and only heard about it once before.

My personal opinion which I expressed to my friend was that Christianity is not about religion but relationship, therefore instead of getting caught up by old religious practices, we should participate in communion which is focused on two emblems, the bread and wine.[109] By placing emphasis on foot washing we've allowed ourselves to get distracted by something that should never have become the primary focus.

---

[109] 1 Corinthians 11:23-26 (NIV)

Appendix: Path to Salvation

We as Christians can be hypocrites; I know that full well because I sometimes have double standards for how I live my life. What saddened me about my friend was that he was so caught up about feet washing that he refused communion; but didn't practice tithing; didn't keep a prayer diary; and scarcely read the Bible. Before I'd discovered this I would quote scriptures all the time throughout our conversation, only to discover that he didn't know what or where I was quoting from. I believe that more important than the act of communion is relationship and that God would want His son to pray daily, read and meditate on the word much more than taking the small piece of bread and wine.

Let's consider for a moment those parts of the world where abject poverty prevents residents from washing feet, let alone acquiring bread and wine. Would that fact make them any less Christian? I don't think so, because what they would have in common with my friend was their ability to pray; and if they were literate and had a Bible, they could read the word of God even in the absence of food on their table.

Many Christians rob God of their time and of His money.[110] When I discussed tithing with my friend, he told me that since he was unemployed he gave only an offering. Maybe it is the lawyer in me, but I have a habit of challenging people, so I asked him, "For the last six years I have had no job, do you think it's okay for me

---

[110] "Will a mere mortal rob God? Yet you rob me. "But you ask, 'How are we robbing you?' "In tithes and offerings ... you are robbing me." Malachi 3:8-9 (NIV)

not to tithe? What if I never got a job? So, I should never tithe?" He couldn't actually answer me right away but when he eventually did, he agreed that I should tithe if I'd been out of work for six years.

At the end of the day like I explained to him, there is a promise in the second part of the scripture *"'and see if I will not throw open the floodgates of heaven and pour out so much blessing that there will not be room enough to store it.'"*[111] If I never tithed 10% of my 'income' I would never experience the blessings that God has promised, consequently even in my unemployed status I tithe 10% of everything I get, birthday money, Christmas money etc. and I can honestly say that I continually reap the rewards financially, with my health etc.

Living Godly requires the removal of certain vices, the distancing from harmful relationships and the immersion in things of Christ. This includes the music you listen to, the films you watch, and even the books you read. Growing in your walk is relatively easy because everything is readily available with social media, the T.V. and radio.

I do not endorse any televangelists, preachers or authors because there is so much compromise; prosperity preaching and the like. I do not read Christian books anymore but make an exception if the subject matter concerns relationships and dating. Despite this and the fact that the Table of Contents of one such book

---

[111] *Supra* 67

inspired me to write this chapter, I am unwilling to recommend any titles here. All I will mention on this subject is that the Bible advocates sex after marriage not before, between one man and one woman.[112] The Song of Solomon is a book in the Bible centered wholly on sex inside marriage since sex was designed by God and not just for procreation.

My advice where Christian relationships are concerned:

1. *Keep it public*

- o Avoid spending time together anywhere dark and/or secluded
- o Spend time together in groups
- o NEVER go to your boyfriend or girlfriend's home
- o The bedroom is out of bounds

2. *Don't go horizontal*

- o Whether you're watching a movie or just hanging out
- o Always remain vertical

3. *Have an accountability partner*

- o Make sure they are the same gender as you and that you feel comfortable sharing with them in complete transparency

---

[112] *"But since sexual immorality is occurring, each man should have sexual relations with his own wife, and each woman with her own husband."* 1 Corinthians 7:2

o It would also be advisable that they have been a Christian longer than you and are living a sexually pure life as a single or married individual (if they are married they are not engaging in extra marital relations)

4. Don't have late night chats

o People call it 'The Witching Hours.' Keep your conversations to day time hours to avoid the temptation of breaching into phone sex

5. Refrain from any physical contact

o Discuss if holding hands is a safe boundary for you both

o Limit to side hugs only

o Definitely NO kissing

This is not an exhaustive list of guidelines but just a general idea. The most important thing to do is have a conversation with each other. Communication is crucial to maintaining sexual purity, because you may inadvertently do something that tempts your boyfriend or girlfriend, so you need to be bold enough to talk about these things. The best sex is in marriage so wait until your wedding day.

I hold a firm belief that Christianity is about relationship and not religion. Consequently I believe that everything in its natural state is good. Let me explain:

1. Marijuana in its natural state is a plant until it is modified and smoked

2. Tobacco in its natural state is a plant until it is manufactured into cigarettes

3. Grapes in its natural state are a fruit, until it is fermented to produce alcohol; excessive consumption causes intoxication and the loss of inhibitions

4. Sex in its natural state between one husband and his one wife honors God, it dishonors God when it is done in pornography or between a child and an adult, with animals or between family members

5. Exercise in its natural state is good, but engaging in yoga, Pilates or Zumba dishonors God

In my opinion what was originally good was distorted by Satan. Marijuana, tobacco, grapes and sex are not sins in their natural state; it is only once they are distorted that they become sinful and dishonoring to God.

I believe that there is no hard and fast rule to living the life of a Christian. What I can say is that Christians are imperfect people serving a perfect God who transforms their heart and mind. He accepts you exactly as you are[113] and will transform you to become more like Him. Bearing that in mind, I feel that Christians need to stop judging one another. First of all, not every human being struggles with sexual sin. Second since

---

[113] *"When Jesus heard this, He told them, "Healthy people don't need a doctor – sick people do. I have not come to call the righteous, but sinners." Mark 2:17 (NIV)*

Jesus takes us as we are, people in church may indeed initially still struggle with lust, fornication, alcoholism, pornography etc.

The way I look at it is like this, when you put seeds into a plant pot, the seeds will grow. One day the plant would bud and rise above the surface of the soil, but it would be so small that you would not actually see it until it grew big enough to be visible to the naked eye.

In the same way, we as Christians will have struggles and battles with sin[114] but I believe that change would take place albeit gradually. An example is a person smoking cigarettes that has given their life to Christ but not yet kicked the habit. Since our *"bodies are temples of the Holy Spirit,"*[115] we should not destroy it internally or externally.

What I sometimes picture is a person who smoked twenty cigarettes a day and is now down to ten. For those of us who are judgmental we are just going to see the fact that the individual smokes not their reduction. I therefore encourage you to always think of the growth of a plant from seeds until it produces buds and then transforms to full blossom and beauty.

So, what about tattoos? Remember that the body is a temple.[116] Let's think about a beautiful temple in Thailand. Whenever someone visits that temple they

---

[114] *"The spirit is willing, but the flesh is weak."* Matthew 26:41 (NIV)

[115] 1 Corinthians 6:19 (NIV)

[116] *Ibid.*

have to behave in reverence and respect which includes covering their arms and legs just to get inside. The atmosphere and even the noise level stimulate a place of prayer and worship. Now consider for a moment that somebody got paint and decorated the outside walls of the temple, maybe with their name or that of a significant other, what about a pretty star, butterfly or if they were Christian a cross or Bible scripture.

In a country such as Thailand if anyone had the courage to 'decorate' the outside of one of the temples they would be thrown in jail, or worse. If such extreme measures would be taken for a temple of gold why do we consider our bodies to be of less value?

Although many Christians do not like the Old Testament especially the book of Leviticus it is relevant here because it says, *"Do not cut your bodies for the dead, and do not mark your skin with tattoos."*[117] Whether you agree with me or not I am just repeating what the Bible says.

The Bible is our manual and not a guideline book as some people refer to it. It is our Basic Instructions Before Leaving Earth, therefore the most important book that we could read. Someone once asked me which books I had read that had grown my faith; I responded that I read the Bible. I believe that the Bible is more than enough, therefore if a church supplements their teaching or outright endorses or encourages you

---

[117] Leviticus 19:28 (NIV)

to spend equal amounts of time reading the Bible in addition to another book or books by a single author I would have questions about that.

Please understand that a church may have study groups where a book is read and discussed. I have no issues with that at all; my concern is when that book is given equal or greater value to the Bible. There are a number of denominations that supplement their reading with a specific book and are sadly labeled by many outsiders as being a cult. I'm unwilling to discuss this any further, suffice to say, do your own research.

Research is a necessity in life but is often considered to have very little importance to the average man or woman. God encourages us to test the spirit[118] which should be applied both inside and outside of church. Christianity has never been about blind faith but about being fully informed.

Thus far I've had the privilege of travelling to twenty-nine countries. In all of my journeys I have met hundreds of people who all had different experiences. Outside of India I have met very, very few people who had ever visited there (excluding those of Indian heritage of course). It is interesting that considering this fact, I meet plenty of people who believe that they know more about yoga than I do despite never having visited India.

---

[118] *"Beloved, believe not every spirit, but try the spirits whether they are of God: because many false prophets are gone out into the world."* 1 John 4:1 (KJV)

Appendix: Path to Salvation

Having done my research and visited the country multiple times I can say with complete certainty that yoga does not honor God and should not be engaged in by Christians.

The Bible says, be in the world and not off the world.[119] I have always considered this fact that if everyone in the World was doing it than I was going to do the opposite. Therefore when everyone was watching Harry Potter, I abstained; when everyone was getting tattoos, I abstained; when everyone was shaving half their head and covering one of their eyes with their hair, I abstained. Likewise since the world has taken yoga by storm, I abstain.

An article I read once described it best, it went something like this, "If you go into a mosque and say "Jesus, Jesus, Jesus" the mosque doesn't suddenly become a church. In the same way, you cannot expect that by chanting something else whilst performing yoga will change the fact that you're engaging in a Hindu practice and your positions are forms of worship to their gods."

Please understand just because something feels good does not make it right. Yoga is real and is not just some innocent form of exercise. In fact, in the early days yoga was used to introduce people to the Hindu religion. Again, do your research, don't just blindly follow the world even if they Christianize something. You can't Christianize yoga, in the same way you can't

---

[119] *"Love not the world, neither the things [that are] in the world. If any man love the world, the love of the Father is not in him."* 1 John 2:15 (KJV)

Christianize 666, or the name Satan, or the pentagram.

In all things you need God's discernment because as you can see making a commitment to follow Christ isn't the end but is only just the beginning. My desire is that the information you've been given here has not frightened or overwhelmed you; I've simply tried to ensure that you are as informed as possible.

I wholeheartedly believe that these dozen or more pages are my God inspired writings despite it being the early hours of the morning. I do not believe in coincidences, but my book was completed just after lunch on the August 31st, 2018; due to some delays outside of my control I could not submit my manuscript for publication. Saturday morning, I had a television interview which was delayed, and then again due to circumstances outside of my control - this time my inability to get into the house, plus an impromptu opportunity for a speaking engagement - I arrived home too late to submit my manuscript.

On Sundays I generally do not do anything work related because I believe that it is the day of rest. The Ten Commandments instructs us to keep the Sabbath day holy[120] which is a scripture that causes much division between some denominations. The belief in some churches is that the Sabbath is on Saturday, whilst others believe it is on Sunday.

---

[120] *"Remember the Sabbath day, to keep it holy."* Exodus 20:8 (KJV)

I personally don't think it matters. In my opinion so long as you observe a day of rest that is all that really matters Fighting over whether it is a Saturday or Sunday is irrelevant in the big scale of things because once again, God is looking at our hearts.[121]

Again, as I said earlier I believe that Christianity is about relationship not religion or laws. Just as Jesus explained in the Bible "If your donkey falls into a well on the Sabbath will you leave him there?"[122]

I was talking to a friend who explained that he was unable to get a job because he observed the Sabbath from Friday sundown to Saturday sundown. I asked him, "If you got sick on the Sabbath, what would you do, stay home instead of going to the hospital? Since the people in the hospital should be observing Sabbath too and not providing you emergency care." He actually agreed and said he wouldn't go to the hospital but would rather die.

I think such a decision would be foolish. The Bible says, "Obedience is better than sacrifice."[123] I consider it this way, God wants your obedience, but not to the point where you sacrifice your life instead of seeking medical attention. In my opinion that is not wisdom at all, and

---

[121] *Supra* 43

[122] *"Which of you shall have an ass or an ox fallen into a pit, and will not straightway pull him out on the Sabbath day?"* Luke 14:5 (KJV)

[123] *"Does the Lord delight in burnt offerings and sacrifices as much as in obeying the Lord? To obey is better than sacrifice…."* 1 Samuel 15:22 (NIV)

I believe was the point Jesus was trying to get across when he was being questioned for healing people on the Sabbath.[124]

I do not make a practice of working on Sundays but have done so many times in the past. Again, I believe that is where the application of wisdom comes in. I see no sense in behaving like my friend and complaining that you cannot get a job when you are unwilling to make the necessary compromise to obtain employment. I believe God would frown upon such behavior because you'd be using religion as an excuse to remain lazy and idle. God advocates work which we see in the Garden of Eden where he gave Adam the job of naming the animals[125] (just a note guys, before Eve came into the picture, Adam had a job).

Now let's consider a place such as an orphanage. If we strictly observe abstaining from work on the Sabbath who would feed and care for the babies in an orphanage? No one! This is where the application of common sense applies because we cannot become so caught up with religion that we make decisions that are harmful to others.

What I think is really important to note is that even

---

[124] *"And the ruler of the synagogue answered with indignation, because that Jesus had healed on the Sabbath day, and said unto the people, There are six days in which men ought to work: in them therefore come and be healed, and not on the Sabbath day."* Luke 13:14 (KJV)

[125] *"And Adam gave names to all cattle, and to the fowl of the air, and to every beast of the field; but for Adam there was not found a helper suitable for him."* Genesis 2:20 (KJV)

with the creation of the world;[126] God worked before He rested. In the same way I think it's important for us as Christians to get our priorities straight and instead of being so fixated on the Sabbath, we become fixated on working, following which we will then deserve and be entitled to rest.

I hope that gives you some food for thought, and since we are on the subject of 'food' I don't want to omit some discussion on fasting. Fasting is when we abstain from food and sometimes drink including water. During a fast, we as Christians dedicate our time to prayer. I heard that during the years described in the Bible (way before the invention of microwaves,) meals took so many hours to prepare, that when they fasted it freed up surplus time which they devoted to prayer.

Like someone once told me, "Skipping meals is not fasting." I found that statement funny but true because I had observed a friend of mine doing exactly that. He was on a three day fast without food or water; and complained to me that he might pass out. I told him that wisdom was to drink water since passing out and dying was not the smart thing to do.

The Bible is clear that when we fast, we should not beat our chests[127] a.k.a complain. It should be private and intimate between you and God. Observing my friend's

---

[126] *"In the beginning God created the heaven and the earth."* Genesis 1:1 (KJV)

[127] *"When you fast, do not look somber as the hypocrites do, for they disfigure their faces to show others they are fasting.... But when you fast ... wash your face, so that it will not be obvious to others that you are fasting."* Matthew 6:16-18 (NIV)

abstention from food and water it seemed to me as though he was trying to manipulate God. He told me that he would continue fasting until God answered his prayer; but the interesting thing was that instead of spending the time in quiet devotion or prayer with God, he was hanging out and socializing with me at the beach, minus his Bible.

Skipping meals does not get God's attention but our obedience to Him does; the submission of our will to His will! After the three day fast, my friend did not get the results that He wanted. Why? In my opinion because God is not Santa Claus that we can manipulate for what we want with our sometimes foolish actions.

God is such a good God that there have been times I have merely had a thought and He answered my 'prayer.' We cannot twist the hand of God with our action or inaction, and honestly why should we?

I just want to challenge you here that whenever you do embark on a time of prayer and fasting that you test your motives and consider what you are trying to accomplish. Are you merely skipping meals or entering into a time of sacrifice and devotion?

So, as I was saying earlier, generally speaking I do not work or write my book on Sundays (although I frequently volunteer on Sundays) but on the evening of September 2nd things were a little different. After enjoying my second day at the beach in more than three months, I settled in to read a Christian dating book. Before I could complete reading page three I was so inspired by the Table of Contents that I began writing this Appendix.

Unlike the previous nights, my host was home from work but this time with her bedroom door open. The walls were thin thus any noise would travel even further because of her open door. She was on and off the phone between the hours of 8.30 p.m. and 1.30 a.m. which had never happened before. The noise would have made it impossible for me to sleep but I was otherwise occupied and focused. That entire night I sat typing as the words kept flowing minus the usual interruptions of attacking mosquitoes.

I am 100% convinced that this appendix needs to be here even if I am breaking all the rules of authorship. The Bible says that we must be fishers of men,[128] so if I do not use this medium to actively share the gospel than I have fallen short and lost an opportunity to extend the invitation of salvation that I once received.

This invitation is available to all, and it's yours for the taking with those simple steps of *ABC: Admit, Believe, Confess.*

---

[128] *"Follow me, and I will make you fishers of men."* Matthew 4:19 (KJV)

Resources

Cambodia

AFESIP-Cambodia

AFESIP-Cambodia was established in 1996, by Somaly Mam (herself a victim of trafficking), to combat human trafficking and sexual exploitation of women and children. Through its work it addresses all of the consequences of human trafficking, including preventative measures aimed at reducing the demand for further victims of human trafficking and in turn challenging gender-based-violence and addressing this as a human rights issue.

AFESIP-Cambodia works with young women and girls who are victims or at risk of being victims of sex trafficking, violence, abuse, rape, indentured slavery or exploitation and their families to provide safety and sustainable exit strategies. AFESIP-Cambodia also works closely with government officials, NGO's, community leaders and international partners to address the issues involved.

Sao Chhoeurth, Program Director
afesip.org
afesip.nc@gmail.com

289

Phone: +855 1288 8840

Chab Dai

Chab Dai is committed to addressing human trafficking and exploitation through facilitation of cross-sector and multi- organizational collaboration and improving the capacity of stakeholders through technical training, program support and organizational development.

---

chabdai.org
info@chabdai.org
Phone: +1 916-932-204 / +1 866 305-9800

Daughters of Cambodia

To enable [prostituted women] to exit the sex industry permanently, by providing services that empower them internally; to provide employment; to develop small businesses; to facilitate holistic recovery through treatment and care (medical, psychological and social), creative classes and life skills education; to teach girls to make and sustain healthy choices and be responsible for their lives; to achieve professionalism as an organization; and to disciple girls who become Christians to follow Jesus Christ and experience [a transformed] life at the deepest levels through outworking their faith in Jesus .

---

daughtersofcambodia.org

office@daughtersofcambodia.org
Phone: +855 8 991 0203

She Rescue Home

The SHE Rescue Home is an aftercare facility for girls under 16 who have been trafficked, raped, prostituted or are at risk.

Tim Hughes, Country Director
sherescuehome.org
tim@sherescuehome.org

India

Freedom Firm

The Mission: Rescue, Restoration and Justice

Freedom Firm seeks to eliminate child prostitution in India by rescuing minor girls, providing effective rehabilitation and prosecuting the perpetrators of sex trafficking.

Rescue - Freedom Firm undercover operatives locate minor girls in brothels and document the crime. This information is then reported to the police. The Freedom Firm team, along with the police, raid the brothels, rescue the girls and arrest the brothel keepers and traffickers. The rescued girls are then placed in government remand homes and Freedom Firm files criminal complaints against their oppressors.

Restoration - Freedom Firm's social workers partner with shelter homes across the country to provide rescued girls with counseling, therapy, job training, education and health care. The creative program includes a summer camp, animal therapeutic activities with partner organization Leg Up, and employment with business Ruhamah Designs to help the girls grow in confidence and independence.

Justice - Freedom Firm actively pursues the conviction of those responsible for trafficking minor girls. Freedom Firm lawyers assist public prosecutors at each stage of the criminal trial. Rescued girls are empowered to testify against their abusers and to help bring them to justice. Every trial and every conviction creates a deterrent and raises the cost of sex trafficking in India.

Greg Malstead, Co-Founder
freedomfirm.org
Phone: +91 423 244 3053 (India) +1 720 432 1607 (USA)

Global Concerns India

Global Concerns India is a community based, not-for-profit registered organization, working on [the] human rights of women and children from impoverished, vulnerable communities. They believe in investing in people, to encourage each one to be their own first line of defense. To this effect, they engage children, youth, women and men towards becoming leaders with values. They work in combating human trafficking for the purposes of sexual exploitation and bonded labor. [They also facilitate the] education of children and women.

Their programs are with all sections and walks of people, towards making their villages and cities safer. Collaborating with government and like-minded CSOs form part of their ideology, to build collectives that will together stand side by side to make women and children powerful human beings willing to dream, aspire and inspire.

Brinda Adige, Founder and Mentor
brindaadige@gmail.com /
globalconcernsindia@gmail.com
globalconcernsindia.org
Phone: +91 9845518138 / 080-22211548

Philippines

ECPAT Philippines

ECPAT Philippines is a global network of organizations and individuals working together for the elimination of child prostitution, child pornography and the trafficking of children for sexual purposes. It seeks to encourage the world community to ensure that children everywhere enjoy their fundamental rights free and secure from all forms of commercial sexual exploitation.

ecpatphil@gmail.com

ecpatphilippines.org
Phone: +632 9208 151

PACT

PACT envisions itself as a leading network of advocates for child protection against trafficking in the Philippines.

---

philippinecampaign@gmail.com
pact.org.ph
Phone: +632 929 0347

Visayan Forum

VF is a non-profit, non-stock and non-government organization in the Philippines established in 1991. VF works for the welfare of marginalized migrants, especially those working in the invisible and informal sectors, like domestic workers, and trafficked women and children.

It is licensed and accredited by the Department of Social Welfare and Development (DSWD) to provide "residential care and community-based programs and services for women and children in especially difficult circumstances."

It is most known for its pioneering and documented work on domestic workers in the Philippines, especially in pushing for the Domestic Workers Bill or the Batas Kasam bahay. It is also in the forefront of providing services to trafficking victims by managing Halfway

Houses constructed by the Philippine Ports Authority in major Philippine ports and the Manila International Airport Authority.

---

director@visayanforum.org
visayanforum.org
Phone: +63 2 709-0711

United States

Airline Ambassadors International

Airline Ambassadors International (AAI) was founded to leverage airline connections to help vulnerable children but after correctly identifying human trafficking on four airlines in 2009, AAI has become a leading advocate for awareness of human trafficking in the aviation industry.

Nancy Rivard, President and Founder
nancy@airlineamb.org
airlineamb.org
Phone: +1 866 264-3586

Apne Aap Women Worldwide

Their mission is to increase choices for at-risk girls and women in order to ensure access to their rights, and to deter the purchase of sex through policy and social change.

Prof. Ruchira Gupta, Founder and President
apneaap.org

Freedom Ladder

Freedom Ladder is a global nonprofit organization dedicated to making the world safe for children by educating them about the issues that are important to their lives using popular entertainment. They partner with law enforcement agencies, child welfare organizations, and entertainment artists to design effective tools with captivating narratives that inspire young people to be the primary agents in their own self-protection and personal flourishing.

Their accompanying entertainment website reinforces and expands these life lessons. They distribute their innovative educational tools online and through schools, youth organizations, faith communities, law enforcement agencies and other organizations and individuals who care about the welfare of young people. Their mission is to inspire young people to live lives of safety, courage, and inspiration.

Thomas Estler, Founder and Director
freedomladder@gmail.com abolitionista.org
Phone: +1-917-696-0112

Love Justice International

Through transit monitoring and interception, They attack trafficking at the most strategic moment—

while it is in the process of occurring and BEFORE exploitation and enslavement. They have intercepted over 15,000 people from slavery, exploitation, and abuse. Throughout the developing world, children are cast aside by poverty, war, and the destruction of families.

They serve these orphaned children by placing them in loving homes before they are subject to the devastation of the trafficking industry, drug trade, or disease. They believe in the life-changing impact of education. Through their Dream School, they help children realize their dreams by fostering an environment where they can become all God has created them to be.

Doug Dworak, Executive Director
lovejustice.ngo

Million Kids

Million Kids works with local law enforcement and concerned citizens, businesses, and organizations to end human trafficking domestically. Locally, they serve on the Riverside County Anti-Human Trafficking Task Force (RCAHT). They help activists and communities develop effective anti-trafficking programs in their locales. They educate and engage individuals, organizations and corporations about human trafficking. Internationally, they conduct programs and work with partners to serve rescued children and to create prevention strategies. They provide local solutions while taking a global perspective on the human trafficking problem.

Opal Singleton, President and CEO
Opal@MillionKids.org
MillionKids.org
ExploitedCrimes.com

National Law Center for Children and Families

Since 1991, the National Law Center has been protecting children from sexual exploitation by training and equipping Law Enforcement Officers and prosecutors across America with the most cutting edge investigative strategies to prevent, detect, and successfully prosecute crimes against children, especially online luring and technology-facilitated crime.

For many years, the NLC has been producing extensive legal materials, national guidance and training in the area of child sexual exploitation law. NLC PROTECTS Seminars prominently feature national experts on child pornography investigation and prosecution, Internet forensics, online enticement investigation, human trafficking, and other child sexual exploitation issues.

Larry Dershem, Esq. President

ldd@nationallawcenter.org
nationallawcenter.org
Phone: +1 703 548 5522

National Human Trafficking Hotline

The National Human Trafficking Hotline is a national anti- trafficking hotline serving victims and survivors of human trafficking and the anti-trafficking community in the United States. The toll-free hotline is available to answer calls from anywhere in the country, 24 hours a day, 7 days a week, every day of the year in more than 200 languages.

Their mission is to provide human trafficking victims and survivors with access to critical support and services to get help and stay safe, and to equip the anti-trafficking community with the tools to effectively combat all forms of human trafficking. They offer round-the-clock access to a safe space to report tips, seek services, and ask for help. They also provide information, statistics, and resources on a wide range of topics related to human trafficking.

---

help@humantraffickinghotline.org
humantraffickinghotline.org
Phone: + 1-888-373-7888 / Text 233733

Polaris Project

Polaris is a leader in the global fight to eradicate modern

slavery. Named after the North Star that guided slaves to freedom in the U.S., Polaris systemically disrupts the human trafficking networks that rob human beings of their lives and their freedom. Their comprehensive model puts victims at the center of what they do – helping survivors restore their freedom, preventing more victims, and leveraging data and technology to pursue traffickers wherever they operate.

info@polarisproject.org
polarisproject.org
Phone: +1 202-745-1001

Shared Hope International

Shared Hope International strives to prevent the conditions that foster sex trafficking, restore victims of sex slavery and bring justice to vulnerable women and children. It provides comprehensive research, expert testimony, coalition support and advocacy initiatives that strengthen trafficking laws and build better policies in order to protect victims and prosecute traffickers, buyers and facilitators.

savelives@sharedhope.org
sharedhope.org
Phone: +1 866-437-5433

SOLD

SOLD, a moving account of child trafficking based on

research in the brothels of Calcutta.

Patricia McCormick, Author
pattymccormick.com
soldthemovie.com/trailers/
soldthemovie.com/screenings/

World Childhood Foundation (WCF)

WCF envisions a world where all children are free from violence, sexual abuse, and exploitation. Founded in 1999 by H.M. Queen Silvia of Sweden, WCF supports the development of solutions to prevent and address violence, defend children's rights, and promote better living conditions for children. It has supported over 1000 projects in 25 countries.

A United Nations accredited NGO, WCF raises awareness about child sexual abuse through programmatic support, global advocacy initiative #EyesWideOpen (co-founded by H.R.H. Princess Madeleine) and high-level meetings with government, academic, civil society, and private sector leaders. In 2016-2017, the WCF served over 73,000 clients—both directly and indirectly—in the United States alone and launched the Stewards of Children Prevention Toolkit mobile app (www.socapp.org) in partnership with Darkness2Light and Ericsson. Childhood USA is a board member of the Global Partnership to End Violence Against Children (http://www.end-violence.org).

Nicole G. Epps, Managing Director
childhood-usa.org
Phone: +1 212 867 6088

REVEALED:
6 Strategies to
Surviving Jail Time

◆

If you're not yet had the opportunity to read the iwitness news article[129] I'd recommend you stop reading and do that right now.

Okay, now, that we have gotten that preliminary out of the way and you have heard figuratively speaking directly "from the horse's mouth" the stage is properly set.

I am sure you have lots of unanswered questions, many of which will not be answered here, but instead will be available in my upcoming book: *Attorney Behind Bars (ABB)/One Smooth Stone.*

With plenty of time on my hands it seemed only fitting that I write not just one but two books about my false imprisonment.

You reading this book means that it was time well spent, that my experience was not wasted, because the

---

[129] News Admin, "Court orders British lawyers deportation", *Iwitness*, June 18 2021. https://www.iwnsvg.com/2021/06/18/court-orders-british-lawyers-deportation-video

information written here is my opportunity to impart my knowledge to you, in the unlikely event that you end up behind bars.

As a law-abiding citizen, Christian, and attorney, that has never worked illegally, I never envisioned being imprisoned on false grounds for the mere fact that I did not want to leave the country but instead acquire temporary residency and eventually make a life for myself there.

These are the six strategies I implemented in surviving jail time:

1. Memorize Choruses and Songs

The Bible says, *"Train up a child in the way he should go and when he gets older, he will not depart."*[130] There is never a truer statement than this, which I can firsthand attest to.

When the door was sealed shut of the jail and I had made myself acquainted with the confined surroundings, armed with 2 books, the Bible, and some vegan reading (*How Not to Die*) all I could do was sing.

The problem was, I had forgotten all the lyrics of the first verses of each song, but I did remember the choruses. Truth be told, it was a bit on the repetitive side, but I had simply had a mental block. Is that any surprise though, considering my circumstances?

---

[130] *"Train up a child in the way he should go, And when he is old he will not depart from it."* Proverbs 22:6 KJV

Obviously not. I, of course, cannot speak for every jail inmate, but what I can say is that even in those first few hours when my liberty and freedom were taken away from me, being able to recite uplifting and God-honoring songs enabled the time to pass.

Now, for those not of the Christian faith, or of a different faith altogether, my advice remains the same. That is not to say that I'm giving you homework to memorize positive songs in the highly unlikely event that you are arrested falsely or otherwise, but it's merely a useful suggestion that you would certainly thank me later, because, God forbid, you land up in jail and don't know the lyrics of any songs you are completely limited to humming and adlibbing the words or nursery rhymes that you were taught back at school, like "Ba, ba black sheep," which in this day and age is probably now deemed as wholly inappropriate, discriminatory and outright racist.

Irrespective of that fact, when you consider on average a song album could run anywhere between 30 minutes to an hour then it is evident that it is definitely an effective way to pass the time which in jail you will have plenty of.

2. Carry a Book

Now, this, at face value, probably sounds incredibly farfetched. Am I actually suggesting that you carry a 500-page book like *"How Not to Die"* around with you? Obviously not and depending on the situation of your arrest this advice may not apply.

However, if you are the subject of deportation proceedings in Saint Vincent and the Grenadines and leniency is allowed, then you would definitely want a book. On the other hand, if it is allowed for someone to bring you a book, newspaper, or some other reading material you should definitely jump at the opportunity.

I can guarantee that you would not regret it, even more so in this digital age where books in print are almost extinct. The great thing about a hardback or paperback is that neither requires batteries or electricity, and from my own experience of visiting prisons, from behind the prison bars, inmates do have access to reading material.

The big question is whether you can actually focus on what you are reading which I found a particularly hard task during the first 4 days of my incarceration. This was due to a number of factors including the book content: health and science, which you will have to forgive me for saying is generally boring on an average day, but even more so when the days are long and arduous in a jail cell.

Do not misunderstand me please, I had thoroughly enjoyed the first 27 pages of *How Not to Die*, it made me laugh and smile, but reading about why turmeric is good for the prevention of cancer just really was not doing it for me, whilst sat in a St Vincent jail cell.

So as practical as it seemed, something a little light-hearted would have been a better deal. This meant that although I had the Bible in tow I still stuck to the formality of my twice daily reading. I say that to say, when considering the nature of your circumstances, that is being incarcerated, in addition, to the encouragement that can be found in religious and Christian scriptures, having an additional book will surely do you the world of good.

So carry your Bible, if available and read and study it, and acquire another book, practically any book. It will help you to focus on something other than your circumstances.

3. Writing Materials

Naturally, having materials that enable you to write is another productive use of time. With all the endless time stretching out ahead of you a lot of which will be spent in your mindless thoughts, the ability to write it all down to make sense of everything will surely go a long way in enabling you to separate beneficial thinking from nonsense.

In fact, I recall meeting a prison inmate during one of my human trafficking prevention presentations who had learned to read and write in prison and composed 76 songs about Jesus. He also had pages and pages of writing about the Bible, complete with various scriptures.

One particular page that comes to mind contained the following: Yahweh can free you from dark web, pornography, addiction, and bad attitude. Whenever I would share that in church there would always be a resounding amen.

Can You Keep A Secret?

Interestingly enough 3 weeks prior to my false imprisonment I had been told repeatedly by a number of people within the space of 24 hours that I should write a book. Now, I was already the author of *CYKAS: Can You Keep A Secret?*, but these people were referring to a book about my life as a missionary.

Now, although I agreed with the advice, I was not in the frame of mind to start writing, so although I made multiple sincere promises to myself that I would write I did not even bother.

Of course, when I got thrown in jail, but given the privilege of having access to pen and paper, I knew exactly what I needed to do (when I was not singing hymns of fellowship). I was going to start writing my new book, and, no it was not about being a missionary but instead being an attorney behind bars (ABB).

As you may have noticed, I have the whole acronym thing going on, first with *CYKAS* and then now with *ABB*. So, despite the mulling backwards and forwards that was the conclusion that I came to, the prequel to the completed product with the working title: *Innocence Looks Like Guilt,* because considering the way in which I was treated, no other book title could truly do my entire experience justice than the use of those words.

This should be a given, but I'll say it anyway, take this opportunity to write letters "home," which doesn't necessarily mean to family or friends, but also mere acquaintances.

In fact, I was indeed the recipient of prison letters

from an inmate, which made me feel valued. My incarceration of course drove home the point that my responses were far too infrequent and should have been on a more consistent basis.

Bearing that in mind, I want to do a little plug here, in case you do not know, but there are organizations and chanties around the world that connect inmates to the general public through a simple and secure letter writing service, which of course I intend to sign up to, you should too.

4. Obtain Contraband: Just Kidding!!

I had to put this one in here, although you are going to have to forgive me for ruining it for the next falsely imprisoned inmate specifically in St Vincent and the Grenadines.

Now, my situation is surely wholly different from any other falsely imprisoned inmate for the mere fact that my story and life were so incredibly unique.

Let me start by saying in all capital letters: **I AM NOT AMERICAN**! I was born in England to Jamaican parents. That makes me British, not English as bizarre as that is, nope I am British, or rather black British to be exact.

Why is that even remotely important? It is because although a licensed N.Y attorney for 7 years, I am UNPAID, yes unpaid. The fancy term is pro bono. It would therefore drive me completely insane when people would constantly mistake me for being

American when I did not remotely look, act, or even sound American.

On the contrary, my accent was a hodge-podge of accents all rolled into just one sentence, and without trying to sound rude, but if I was an American then why was I a free lawyer for the past 7 years?

Well as the saying goes common sense is not common, hence the reason for such a foolish conclusion.

So, now that I have set the record straight, why am I uniquely different? Well, I have just given one reason, coupled with the fact that I was a self-proclaimed missionary, not sent by a church, pastor or organization, but sent by God; add to that my anti-human trafficking work, travelling around the world alone as a public speaker and volunteer completely unpaid.

Clearly money was not my motivation, rather this was a God given calling on my life that sprung out of me surviving childhood sexual abuse from the ages of 4 - 10 by my mother's first husband.

Consequently, in my bid to prevent any other child from enduring such an experience I gave free talks on the aforementioned topics. I say all this to state, on the record, that I was the subject of a witch hunt in St Vincent and the Grenadines for reasons unbeknownst to me.

Arrested; taken to court without any consideration to my dignity; brought in front of the deportation court without my attorney present; and deceptively transported to jail, on what basis?

Because immigration denied my extension citing "9 months is too long for a holiday," and filing deportation paper that I was undesirable because of inadequate finances, despite having in excess of £2000 cash on my person (which the police eventually stole from my belongings) in addition to £10,000 in the bank.

Let me go one step further and share that the immigration officer's affidavit was one document containing my residency application denial (absent a denial reason I should add) and failing to substantiate their claim of insufficient funds.

Suffice to say, the rumor mill was working on overtime, and the court of public opinion had spoken, they wanted me deported and sent home. Why?

My only "crime" was wanting to remain in the country, acquire residency, and work authorization, and build open hiring policy bakeries, hiring ex-convicts. Instead, I was made to feel like an ex-convict and fugitive.

Now, that you understand all of that, let me explain about the contraband because it is probably not what you think.

So, because I was not a criminal in any sense of the word, I was afforded various privileges which included the level of trust that did not include a bodily invasive search.

In addition, I had access to books, writing materials, the communal staff fridge and freezer and my belongings (an entire truckload).

Now, please don't judge me because although my mum will attest to me buying way too much groceries and occupying 2 entire freezers with my vegan junk food substitutes, I had arrived in St Vincent 9 months earlier with 1 suitcase, a carry on and purse, but sitting under the police front desk were 4 boxes, 1 large suitcase (acquired here in the form of a gift), and 13 bags (approximately the average size of the recyclable grocery bags), and to think that immigration claimed that I would become a ward of the state. With that much stuff, I could hardly think so.

I mention all that to say, with so much stuff, plus not being a dangerous criminal, I was given the privilege to access my things and therefore in doing so with careful thought, planning and execution I was able to obtain contraband in the shape of my cellphone, 1 of the 9 cell phones that I had.

Why did I have so many? That is a story for another day. Suffice to say I thank God for the 9 phones including the one with unlimited calls and data that was not in the police's possession.

I did not have to sleep with anyone or bribe anyone, I simply hid it inside my clothes, in the same way that I had hid my pens inside a shirt when they had been confiscated from me the night before and calmly brought them inside my cell, easily done.

Plus, having spent time with prison inmates and staff before in a professional capacity I had witnessed and been told of alcohol, drugs, cigarettes, phones, and a cutlass being found in the inmate cells.

Of course, even if your mission of sneaking in a phone is a success, the next thing to consider is its battery power. As they have yet to invent solar powered cell phones; like me you would have to conserve the battery by minimal usage with data turned off, pre-typed texts before turning on the data and the best suggestion of all is to write your message on paper and take a picture that can in turn be sent by email, using WhatsApp or some other medium.

It means that rather than spending 5 minutes composing a message, you spend less than a minute, snapping a picture of your message and uploading it as an attachment, thus preserving your sacred battery.

Now, pay close attention as I am not, I repeat, not advising you to sneak contraband into jail. Notice the subheading says, "Just kidding."

My situation was a little different because of the circumstances of the false imprisonment. However, as I am sure we all know that contraband is often found in prison cells and not because the inmate sneaked it in under a t-shirt, but rather someone had given it to them.

Oh, and one more thing, if you do somehow get access to a phone behind cell walls you better pray that you have decent signal; but more importantly keep it on silent, not vibrate; reduce the lighting; and make sure you have credit or a suitable phone plan.

5. Regular Visitation

For those of you who are believers, I am sure that you

would never turn down fervent prayer and intercession. Prayer is indeed important, but as the Bible says, "*Faith without work is dead.*"[131] Prayer also requires action and when you are stuck in a jail cell one of the primary things that you will miss is physical contact.

Now, I do not mean sexual intimacy but connecting face to face with another human being (that is not a police or prison officer, who seemingly 99% of the time treats inmates like dirt, which I can attest to from my own firsthand experience).

Having a visitor breaks up the monotony of the day, even more so when it is an attorney-client consultation where you are given a much greater degree of privacy.

Being given access to my phone for an hour in the presence of my attorney was an opportunity I hungered for (even with my contraband device).

Incarceration, like many other life difficulties is the moment when see who your real friends are, and jail often reveals that you have none! Sadly, those you believe have your back, when push comes to shove, they do not, so prepare yourself for victim blaming. That is where they drop out of your life sighting something that you said or did as the reason for their distancing.

My advice to you is, do not take it personally, it is their means of survival and reputation recovery. Instead,

---

[131] *"Even so faith, if it hath not works, is dead,..."* James 2:20 KJV

be open and expect the unexpected because I am convinced that you will be surprised.

The people you least expect to support you, like that odd acquaintance, will. So, where does the church fit into all of this for those of us who are Christian?

Truth be told, I do not know. According to the Bible, Jesus hung out with sinners. Now, let me be clear. He did not engage or endorse their sinful lifestyle. On the contrary, He corrected them in love and empowered them to change. Bearing this in mind, it would be completely reasonable to expect active support from church. In my experience, this was not the case. In fact, the churches I had attended previously made no attempt to contact me, and the church that I had recently begun attending told me they did not support me.

Yes, you heard right. They did not arrange a meeting with me to hear my version of events, instead they relied solely on a heavily government-biased newspaper article; ignorance of immigration laws (which were not available to the public), and their so-called knowledge of such things to make that determination.

Maybe you are reading this and saying with confidence, "My church will be different." But, as the saying goes "Never say never," because when you consider the fact that my only infraction was to stand up in the face of a witch hunt and conspiracy by defying immigration's order to leave the country because "9 months is too long for a holiday," consider for a moment if I had committed an actual criminal offense such as rape or murder. Would that church support me then? The answer is a resounding no.

The Bible says, *"Where does my help come from, does it come from the hills?"*[132] Well, my help was not coming from the hills, from the church, nor any of the entities that I had sacrificed my time to freely educate on human trafficking.

Moral of the story, prepare to be disappointed, but remain positive and hopeful that at least one person will stand in front of you as a visitor.

6. Stay Polite and Positive

Irrespective of your upbringing and the values that your parents instilled in you, common courtesy and respect go a long way. I am sure that we all value warm, good service rather than disrespect and a bad attitude. The dynamics, of course, change when you become an inmate under the authority of the police or prison officers.

What I have personally observed and experienced is the huge power and control domination; being mocked; ignored; ridiculed and bodily harm threatened; all whilst they were on the clock, and despite the fact that I had not been convicted and charged of a heinous crime but was merely under deportation proceedings.

---

[132] *"I will lift up mine eyes unto the hills, from whence cometh my help."* Psalm 121:1

Can you imagine how a prolific sex offender is treated, or how about a serial killer? If society views them as the scum of the earth; then even more so the police and prison officers who may find it their 'ordained' duty and responsibility to make the remainder of that person's life hell.

Jail is not for the faint hearted, or is it? What kept my spirit high was my worship and my thoughts. My mouth was sealed but my head was working on overtime as to how I intended to capitalize on the situation and "become famous."

Ha, ha, ha, well not quite, but after 9 years of unpaid work including 6 years as an unpaid speaker, I had every intention of using this experience as a springboard to propel one into paid overseas, speaking opportunities. If people paid to hear the stories of former prostitutes, then surely, they could pay to hear about my false imprisonment experience too.

Now, I am not saying it is easy being stuck in the confines of four walls like an animal in the zoo, but what I can say is that looking forward (rather than backward) makes a world of difference, even if instead of 6 days, it is 6 weeks, months, or years.

Now, disregarding my earlier statement that 99% of officers treat inmates worse than dogs, that honestly is not true. In my own experience a number of officers came and went, too many to count, but what I can say is that at least 4 of the officers were okay. I say 'okay' because one of them seemed to have an alter ego or split personality, treating me horribly one night and amazingly the next.

The other caused me no issues at all but did not have the decency to address me by name (like all the other staff did). Instead it was "Hello, Hello," and when there was a neighboring inmate I had no clue to whom she was talking.

The third one caused me absolutely no concerns and the 4th was way beyond okay, in fact the nicest member of staff that I had encountered.

What I believe is that they are some members of the prison and police force who set out to break you and destroy your spirit. One such officer, Corp Dragon as I called him launched an unprovoked verbal attack at me, calling me "Wicked," and threatening to punch me. Now, because I do not use expletives, my best retort was "Karma; vengeance is God's; Satan get behind thee," before bursting out in song, at screaming volume, and just as the Bible says, *"Submit yourselves therefore to God. Resist the devil and he will flee from you."*[133] Corp. Dragon walked away.

The next morning when I walked past him to use the toilet, I observed him watching me. He may have tried to destroy my spirit but he categorically failed! Even if

---

[133]   James 4:7 KJV

he took my hymn book, he could never stop me singing. All I did was keep my eyes on the future.

When the power of God is with you, you will have a supernatural strength and ability to go through trials and tribulations laughing. Whether those are all simply internal laughs, on the inside you know that you have already won, that this is only a season and it is temporary.

I say that because the immigration officer who told me that if I piss in the car, I should rub my face in it kept coming to the jail on an almost daily basis including on the weekend in civilian clothes and would always watch me with a great interest.

I did not respect her and could barely open my mouth to greet her, not to mention the fact that she would say "I'm checking how you are?" That was her depraved sick sense of humor since I had a swollen foot, and bad back as a result of the deplorable conditions including a bed that was an upside down, cold wooden table.

Aside from her, who I disliked with a passion, with her false sense of concern. I was very respectful to all the staff. I always said please and thank you, including when they let me back inside the jail cell. I addressed them by name if I knew it, or ma'am or excuse me when I did not. Not once did I cry and on only two occasions was that even a remote possibility.

The first was a short time after I had arrived and was feeling sorry for myself, but I quickly snapped out of it and sang songs. The second time was when I got the news my friend was disowning me (in my opinion because of a bruised ego when she got a message not to discuss anything in front of the police; then feeling slighted she came to the police station and discussed everything in front of them, sigh). Feeling truly abandoned I once again snapped out of it by singing songs.

I was proud of myself for the way I handled it. I sadly did not deserve 10 out of 10 points for losing my temper on the first day (which was wholly justified when the police refused to let me call my lawyer, and mocked and laughed at me saying, "Why do you need a lawyer? You're being deported?" To which I replied that was none of his business); and the second occasion after my former friend told all my business to the police which resulted in the police calling me wicked, a demon and threating to punch me. I would say on both occasions my reaction was definitely warranted, but the way I reacted was not. Of course, I can readily admit that I am not perfect but neither am I worthless, a dog, or the scum of the earth.

The people of St Vincent may disagree but I know who I am and whose I am and that my identity is in Christ. I cannot speak for every man or woman on the earth. But I can say that I am convinced that every one of us has a deep inner strength, something we know nothing about until a time when we are pushed into a situation that allows our strength to shine. When I consider myself and my personality type, I am amazed at how well I handled the situation, and my behavior shocked the guards.

Remember, my mouth was closed and my brain was working on overtime. Of course, not every formerly incarcerated individual will have the ability to share their story, nor the platform. But irrespective of that I think it is vitally important to focus on the future, the things you will do when given the freedom and opportunity to do so; the positive impact your experience can have on another by donating your time and giving back to those in the same position you just left behind.

No matter what the police or prison staff may try they can never harm your mind. There are no limits to where your imagination can take you.

So, what do I envision following my experience? Well a few things:

1. Paid speaking opportunities to share my message and story, educating and empowering nations on human trafficking and child abuse;

2. Financial stability that enables me to be debt free;

3. Financial provision so that I can finally realize my 10-year-old dream of building open hiring policy bakeries hiring ex-convicts;

4. The financial resources to build safe houses in the Philippines for victims of sex trafficking;

5. For my book and message *CYKAS: Can You Keep A Secret?* to go viral, changing the lives of every

parent and child on the topic of sexual abuse around the world;

6. For a husband: Ha, ha, ha. I had to add the last one since this is like my written vision board.

When every one of my 6 dreams become a reality, then this experience would definitely be worthwhile.

In fact, I shared with some friends quite recently that I needed to start advertising and marketing my book and now I had the perfect way of doing so. Although it was hardly a laughing situation, as best as I could I needed to find humor in all that transpired.

No matter how many times I say it, I really want it to sink in, stay positive. In my case, generally speaking I was treated well. It really, could have been so much worse.

For me, putting aside the contraband phone for a moment, my ability to write, read and sing hymns made the world of difference throughout my experience. Unlike the other inmates who slept all day, struggling with severe insomnia my entire life as a result of the trauma I endured as a child victim of incest meant sleeping was just not an option.

So, let us assume I had no pen, paper, hymnal, 500-page book, or Bible then what would I do? Sing choruses and lie down all day pretending to sleep? Not the most ideal, but I would make the best of a bad situation. I truly thank God that was not the case however, because writing 19 pages in a book per day most definitely passed the time.

So, when all is said and done, be prepared, stay positive, remain prayerful, and be polite.

Do NOT resist arrest, doing so gives the police or prison officers all the ammunition they need to brutalize you. "Resist arrest" in the courtroom through the mouthpiece of your lawyer.

One final point I need to add, for those of you on the outside of the prison walls: I desired only temporary residency, a work permit and eventually land to build and open hiring policy bakeries hiring ex-convicts.

I was not given the right to a fair hearing but instead bundled off to jail without ever being heard. These were the 6 things that kept my sanity.

Can You Keep A Secret?

A true story where faith fights human trafficking, corruption, and false imprisonment.

ATTORNEY BEHIND BARS

Inspirational Memoir

JUANITA M. HEADLEY

COMING SOON

About Changing Cases

Changing Cases is the brainchild of Juanita Maud Headley who was born and raised in London, England, by her Jamaican born parents. At the age of seventeen she pursued an international hospitality management Diploma in Switzerland, training as a chef at the United Nations. Juanita's love for food particularly baking and her passion for selflessly helping others saw the birth of Changing Cases, a grassroots organization that wants to incorporate both of her professions as an attorney and a chef.

Changing Cases was founded in 2014, prior to Juanita's first trip of many to the Philippines. The organization aims to achieve the eradication of sexual exploitation and homelessness by building shelters and orphanages, teaching culinary arts, and providing employment for individuals who have been rescued from exploitation or human trafficking.

Changing Cases will eventually also include a bakery with open hiring policy thereby providing jobs for individuals who are homeless, but are of sane mind, men and women who have left the sex industry; and men and women who were formerly incarcerated. This has been and still is a deep desire of its founder who understands that this in itself is a magnanimous undertaking, but she also believes in the fundamental principle that is at the root of Changing Cases, which is that EVERYONE deserves a second chance. This principle that Juanita Headley clings to is fueled by her faith in Jesus Christ who gives a second chance at life to everyone who chooses to accept Him in their heart.

Changing Cases is entirely Nonprofit, and the ultimate goal is for its bakery to also stand in this vain as a charitable establishment with its cakes and baked goods providing the necessary funding for the organizations initiatives.

You have supported the work of Juanita Headley and her Nonprofit Organization Changing Cases because (after a 10% tithe deduction) 50 % of the profits raised from the purchase of this book will go towards supporting these two initiatives. An additional 10% will also be given as commissary to incarcerated individuals, and 10% for the purchase of PPE for Indonesian men who climb the Java volcano collecting Sulphur for $8 a day. You can also show your support by ordering cakes through changingcases.com or by making monetary donations online at changingcases.org. Volunteer support is always greatly needed and appreciated and most importantly of all prayer support.

As the slogan of Changing Cases reads, 'Bake Juan's Way to Change;' you too can change someone's world.

About the Author

Juanita Maud Headley has been a licensed, practicing, volunteer New York attorney since the summer of 2014. She also has a decade of global humanitarian experience which has included disaster relief work, feeding members of the indigent community, serving individuals in the Red Light District and volunteering with juvenile offenders and victims of human trafficking, sexual abuse and exploitation.

Her human trafficking presentations have been heard by individuals at the Office of the Prime Minister in Tobago, by police and army officials in Trinidad and the Philippines and Filipino mayoral officials. She has also been featured on Ghanaian; New York and Trinidadian media outlets.

Having been a victim of childhood sexual abuse she still suffered from the aftereffects of her experience. This, in addition to living abroad unconventionally from December 2012 reshaped the course of her life, including her way of thinking and viewing other people, particularly those deemed to be outcasts of society because of harmful decisions or actions they had made towards themselves or others.

Despite the violations she experienced at such a tender age, Juanita was a firm believer in second chances, which her Christian faith had a lot to do with. Notwithstanding how challenging her living situation tended to be, her life's mission has been to educate and empower people on the scourges of human trafficking and serve the community in whatever way she could.

Juanita continues to travel around the world engaging in public speaking and as an anti-trafficking volunteer primarily in India and the Philippines. For speaking engagements she can be contacted via her website: changingcases.org or by e-mail: Juanita.headley@ changingcases.com